Judy's Copy

Jack Grunthy
Lavender Springs
Feb 1999

HUMAN INTELLECT
AND
THE ORIGIN OF ETHIC

Jack M. Gwaltney, Jr., M.D.

Intellect Books
Free Union, Virginia

Copyright 1997 by Jack M. Gwaltney, Jr., M.D.

All rights reserved. No part of this book may be reproduced in any form or by any means, including photocopying, or utilized by an information storage and retrieval system without written permission from the copyright owner.

Printed in the United States of America

Library of Congress Catalog Card Number 97-94624

ISBN 0-9665684-0-0

My loving thanks to my wife, Sarah Gwaltney and my friends, Robert Abbott, Ph.D., Frederick Hayden, M.D., Owen Hendley M.D., and The Reverend Jane Sigloh for giving of their intellects to improve the book, and to my mother for the final proof reading of the manuscript.

Intellect — The capacity for thought

Webster's Dictionary

This book is dedicated to the human intellect and the belief that acquiring knowledge strengthens intellectual power

Preface

While in the practice of medicine, I have been privileged to know many people and to observe their thinking and behavior from a professional and detached point of view. I have also had the opportunity to conduct investigations in medical science and epidemiology, thus, acquiring some understanding of biology, molecular biology, and causality. In observing human thought and behavior, I have been intrigued with its similarities to that of animals while at the same time, differing in important ways. The recent discovery of certain facts about animal biology and behavior appear to offer new insight into the animal-human relationship, that important subject which continues to stir our emotions. On learning of these new discoveries, I became excited by the possibility that a better understanding might be gained by a systematic review of the known features of animal and human thinking and behavior in the context of the new information. Facts are now available which shed light on critical events in the intellectual separation of higher primates from the other animals and on the separation of humans from higher primates. Viewed in the context of my experience with both the human and animal intellect, this information formed the basis of the conclusions which seem to me probable and are the subject of this work.

The scope of the book precludes it adhering to the traditional standards of academic scholarship. The individual topics included in this book could easily be the subject of extensive works on their own. Also, individual factual statements are not annotated, although important original sources are listed and discussed at the end. Real life and commonplace examples are given to support statements which are so obvious that a formal reference would be gratuitous. Perhaps most importantly, the book was written for people in all stations of life, some of whom might not be attracted to a more formal presentation of the material. Because the subject is important to everyone, it is important that everyone be given the opportunity to understand it. It is my sincere hope that the book will be read and enjoyed by a wide variety of people, especially those who at sometime may have wondered why life was so hard.

In considering the animal-human relationship, we are strongly influenced by the traditional attitudes of our human culture to which we are exposed from birth. As very young children, our emerging intellect is captured by these attitudes and they continue to color our thinking throughout the rest of our lives. It is quite conceivable that someone who has never given serious thought to the subject, reflecting on the manifest differences between animals and humans, would think the subject unworthy of consideration. Nevertheless, such a conclusion, even if well founded in tradition and personal experience, would be unsatisfactory unless it could be shown that the new evidence of genetic relatedness between humans and animals is false. It is true that animals and humans are in many ways quite different, but it is preposterous to rely on characteristics that also vary greatly from one animal species to another while ignoring the new molecular evidence which has proven to have the certainty of life itself. However, the purpose of the book is not to convince the reader of animal-human relatedness, but to examine new facts about that relatedness which help to explain how human intellect evolved and why it is in some ways unique.

It is, therefore, of the highest importance to gain an insight into the factors leading to the development of human intellect as it exists today. Having a long interest in training dogs for retrieving competition, I was informed by a friend that animals did not possess a sense of "reference." That is that animals could not grasp the concept of "more" or "less" as applied to objects and activities. This appeared to explain the observation that retrievers have difficulty in remembering multiple objects placed in certain spatial relationships. I was also aware that animals do not possess self-awareness as manifested by a recognition of their own image in a mirror. It seemed to me probable that these two observations were related. This insight into the importance of self-awareness in affecting certain intellectual functions has afforded a clue about some of the factors responsible for the development of human intellect. It also provids a benchmark for recognizing which types of thought and behavior were present before human intellect reached the stage of development which separated it from that of the animals.

From these considerations, the first section of the book will examine human intellectual function. The first discussion will be devoted to self-awareness in humans and higher primates. I shall demonstrate that other species of animals lack this capacity, and that the development of self-awareness was a necessary, but not sufficient, cause for the development of human intellect in its present state. The discussion will next address the role of self-awareness in fostering an appreciation of the concepts of "standards" and "ideals", this being a unique characteristic of the human intellect. It will then be seen that acquiring the ability to understand standards and ideals gave human intellect its capacity to make conscious judgements, which has led to the development of Ethic and a sophisticated understanding of causation.

The word "Ethic" has been selected to describe the essence of what makes us human, our unique intellectual capability to consciously care about others in the same way that we care about ourselves. The emergence of this singular principle of thought and behavior, familiarly known as "The Golden Rule," will be examined for what it truly was, the signal that *homo sapiens* had become human.

Next, the discussion will turn to the part of intellect associated with our animal origins and to the role of emotion. It will be seen that the continuing animal side of human intellect can be identified as that part responsible for directing all behavior not requiring self-judgement. With this understanding, it will be seen that the uniquely human features of intellect have appeared in only a very recent period in our development. As true humans, we have just been "born." For this reason, dates in the book are given on the 5 million-year time scale over which our species has developed. Most of day-to-day "human" activity as well as emotion are controlled by those parts of intellect that arose during our long animal past. I will then return to the uniquely human qualities of intellect and discuss the appearance of our most advanced intellectual achievements – ethical conduct and the understanding of causation. The origin and workings of Ethic will then be examined, followed by a discussion of the emerging capacity of the human intellect to understand the principles of causality.

At this point, the difficulties in accepting the theory will then be addressed; first, the difficulty in accepting the powerful animal component of human nature; secondly, the persuasiveness of the evidence of human, but not animal, self-awareness; thirdly, the strength of the evidence that animals lack the intellectual capacity for reference; fourthly, the evidence for the existence of unique features of the human intellect, and finally, the question of whether there is evidence to support the concept of free will in human behavior.

The next section of the book will deal with the practice of human behavior: what makes a person human, the personal importance of this knowledge to the individual, the implications for our species, factors which may activate the animal and the human side of intellect, the difficult practical questions which arise when the dual nature of intellect is appreciated, real life behavior, and the important question of can human qualities be consciously developed. Next, the relationship of animal and human behavior to government, education, and training will be considered. I shall then discuss altered function of the intellect which results from mental illness, the use of mind-altering drugs, bureaucracy, entertainment, and fashion.

The next section of the book describes ways in which the intellect may be misled. This will include discussions of lying, seeking "balance", romanticism, artificial communication through the media, intelligence without wisdom, perfectionism, and inadequate self-evaluation. A section then follows in which there is a discussion of the relationship of spirituality and faith to the function of intellect. This includes a reflection on the significance of human self-awareness as interpreted in traditional creation myths compared to its actual importance in human historical development. The final section summarizes the ideas which have been presented in the book. It also contains an epilogue with an actual dialogue about the message of the book. A listing and summary of important sources which support and expand on the ideas in this book are given at the end.

No one should feel surprised that much remains unexplained in regard to the origin and function of human intellect, if due allowance is made for the difficulty in objectively examining one's own self. When looking in a mirror at ourselves, not as we would to groom, but as we might to critically exam another individual, self-recognition is accompanied by shame which makes continued self-examination painful and difficult to endure. In no less way than in visual self-appraisal, intellectual self-evaluation is a difficult and painful undertaking. Seen from this perspective, it is not remarkable that little scientific attention has been given to this subject in relation to its overriding importance to our species. Although much remains and will remain unknown, the evidence now available shows that the view entertained by some – that humans and animals are unrelated – and the view held by others – that humans and animals are equal in their intellectual and ethical capacity – are both erroneous. While I am fully convinced that humans are very closely related to the non-human primates, I am equally convinced that humans are unique because of qualitative differences in intellect. Furthermore, I believe that the emergence of the unique human intellect is the most important and astonishing event which has occurred since the formation of the planet.

This book was written as an attempt to provide enlightenment and to bring behavioral change which can spare and improve life. As a teacher and physician, these have been my two major responsibilities. As a result of the understanding described in this book, I have arrived at certain conclusions about my own behavior and that of others which I find helpful in living my life. This book was written in the hope that these conclusions may be useful to others.

Jack M. Gwaltney, Jr., M.D.
June 1, 1998

■
COVER

Positron emission tomography of the human brain. The red area represents word processing activity occurring in the posterior temporal region. (Courtsey of Drs. Julie Fiez and Mark Raichle)

CONTENTS

Preface i

HUMAN INTELLECTUAL FUNCTION

INTRODUCTION 1
SELF-AWARENESS AND REFERENCE 3
STANDARDS, IDEALS AND JUDGEMENTS 6
THE ANIMAL NATURE OF HUMANS 8
EMOTION 12
THE POSITIVE INTERACTION OF INTELLECT AND EMOTION 18
THE HUMAN NATURE OF HUMANS 20
ETHIC 24
WORKINGS OF ETHIC 29
CAUSALITY 34
DIFFICULTIES OF THE THEORY 40

CONTENTS

PRACTICE OF HUMAN BEHAVIOR

UNDERSTANDING WHAT MAKES A
PERSON HUMAN 54

THE PERSONAL IMPORTANCE
OF THIS KNOWLEDGE 60

IMPLICATIONS FOR OUR SPECIES 62

CONDITIONS AFFECTING
HUMAN BEHAVIOR 64

PRACTICAL QUESTIONS REGARDING
OUR ANIMAL BEHAVIOR 66

EVAUATING BEHAVIOR 69

CAN HUMAN QUALITIES BE
LEARNED? 71

ANIMAL VERSUS HUMAN GOVERNMENT 74

LEARNING, TEACHING, AND
TRAINING 77

FACTORS AFFECTING INTELLECTUAL FUNCTION

PATHOLOGIC THOUGHT AND
BEHAVIOR 80

MIND-ALTERING DRUGS 83

BUREAUCRACY 85

CONTENTS

ENTERTAINMENT AND THE ARTS 89
FASHION 94

WAYS THE INTELLECT IS MISLED

LYING 95
SEEKING BALANCE 97
ROMANTICISM 100
ARTIFICIAL COMMUNICATION 101
INTELLIGENCE WITHOUT WISDOM 105
UTOPIAN PARALYSIS 106
INADEQUATE SELF EVALUATION 108

SPIRITUALITY AND FAITH

SPIRITUALITY 110
FAITH 113
MYTH AND REALITY 116

CONCLUSION

SUMMARY 118
EPILOGUE AND DIALOGUE 123
SOURCES OF INFORMATION 127
INDEX 137

TABLES

1 THE TWO PARTS OF OUR NATURE AND BEHAVIOR 9

2 STAGES OF HUMAN UNDERSTANDING OF CAUSALITY 35

3 COMMUNICATION AND THE AVAILABILITY OF INTELLECTUAL INTERACTION 103

HUMAN INTELLECTUAL FUNCTION

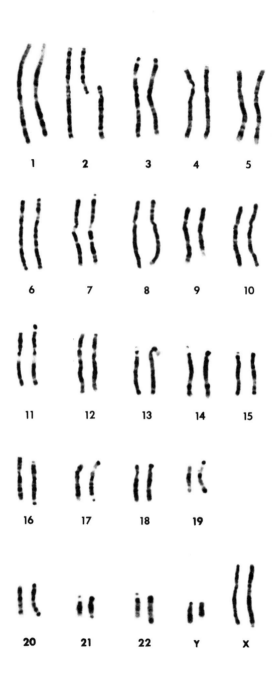

Courtesy of Dr. Jorge Yunis

Introduction

Our Relation to Animals

The animal origin of humans is now a scientific certainty which no intelligent and educated person can fail to appreciate. The scientific certainty of this knowledge is based on chemical evidence provided by our human DNA. Molecular structure is not subject to philosophic debate, and so when analysis of human and chimpanzee genes shows a 99% relatedness between the genic DNA of the two species, the issue is closed – for good. The example on the opposite page shows a comparison of the chromosomes from a human and from a chimpanzee. The human chromosome is the one on the left of each pair and the chimpanzee chromosome is the one on the right.

Our Difference from Animals

And yet the historical record reveals unequivocally that human thought and behavior transcend that of other animals, including the higher primates such as chimpanzees, gorillas, and orangutans, and human brain size is three times that of the apes. We humans moved away from the other higher primates when we consciously developed ethical thinking and behavior and took a second step apart when we began to consciously understand causation and practice science. Nevertheless, the relationship of humans to animals has been a continuing source of confusion and debate. The time has now arrived when it can be understood by all. This book is about how we, as an animal species, became human and what that means.

The Importance of this Understanding

Understanding ourselves, both our unique human characteristics and those shared with animals, is important if we are to prosper as individuals and as a species. Such understanding helps us to develop our human qualities to their fullest while not being misled by the continuing animal side of our nature which, although important to our well-being, is also often destructive. This book was written in the hope that it will be of use to everyone.

Self-Awareness and Reference

People say to each other, "I am I"

Chuang Tzu, 2400 years ago
(4,997,600th Year of Human Origin [HO])

When the people of the world all knew beauty as beauty,
there arose the recognition of ugliness,
When they all knew good as good, there arose the
recognition of evil,
Therefore:
  Being and non-being produce each other;
  Long and short contrast each other;
  High and low distinguish each other.

Lao Tzu, 2600 years ago
(4,997,400 HO)

Self-Awareness and Reference

Self-Awareness in Humans and Apes

Foremost in separating humans and the higher primates from all of the other animal species is the intellectual capacity we possess for self-awareness, for being aware of ourselves and of our own existence. All animals have consciousness – a conscious animal can be rendered unconscious by anesthesia. Only humans and higher primates have self-consciousness, the mental ability to be aware of one's own self. A measure of this difference is that only humans and higher primates have the intellectual capacity to recognize themselves when they see their own image in a mirror. The deceptively simple experiments supporting this discovery have the most profound implications for understanding human thought and behavior. Michael Lewis, a contemporary psychologist who has done pioneering work in the field of the development of self-recognition in children, sees "I am I" as the defining characteristic of self-hood. Two thousand years ago, Chuang Tzu, a Chinese philosopher, used the same expression when grappling with philosophic problems regarding self-awareness.

Self-Awareness is the Foundation of Human Uniqueness

Self-recognition, the *unique* characteristic of humans and higher primates, is the basic intellectual requirement for the development of both philosophical and scientific thinking. Self-recognition is the foundation on which ethical behavior is built, and self-recognition is the starting point for understanding causation and practicing science. Having self-recognition alone, however, has not been sufficient to allow the higher primates to equal these intellectual achievements of humans.

Self-Awareness Allows Understanding of Reference (The Concept of "More" and "Less")

Self-awareness leads to the ability to view things from a perspective which is outside of the usual – animal – perception of the senses. From this vantage point, we can see things in the context of "more" and "less," thus, allowing for a sense of *reference*. Understanding the concept of reference is very important in understanding the ideas in this book. Simple examples are tall-short, hot-cold, near-far, hard-easy, desirable-undesirable and thousands of other examples that we use everyday. Humans make these comparisons automatically and continuously, creating most of the richness of human thought. The development of this understanding is described by the early Chinese philosopher, Lao Tzu, whose words introduce this section.

The way in which humans add reference to their thinking is by using concepts embodied in adjectives, adverbs, and prepositions to qualify objects (nouns) or actions (verbs) – "young man," "beautiful sunset," "pretty girl," "large rock," "walk slowly," "eat quickly," "write clearly," "to town," "away from the fire," "up the stairs." Each modifier implies the existence and understanding of its opposite condition.

Animal Thinking Lacks Reference

To think like an animal, it is necessary to think without employing reference. It means thinking without the ideas and meanings associated with adjectives, adverbs, and prepositions. It means a way of thinking which is restricted to concepts embodied in objects (nouns) and actions (verbs). Of course, even ideas associated with nouns and verbs are severely limited for animals where life is very simple compared to humans. Animals do not know about telescopes, and seed catalogs, and bingo, and computer programming. Examples of basic animal ideas involving actions are things such as "eat," "attack," "submit," "flee," "hide," "have sex," and "romp and play." Basic animal ideas involving things include recognition of specific animals, humans, and objects in their environment. While the number of "noun" and "verb" ideas that humans have compared to animals is enormous, it is not the reason for the *qualitative* difference in the way humans and animals think. Instead, it is the animal's lack of intellectual capacity to make comparisons, the absence of "adjective," "adverb," and "preposition" ideas which makes the difference. For a human, imagining the way an animal thinks is not easy. Human brains automatically add reference to raw sensory information. Because it is so automatic for us to think in this way, it takes a very concentrated and conscious effort to suppress the use of qualifying ideas and to think in the same way as an animal. Try to do it, and you will understand the difficulty.

Standards, Ideals,
and
Judgements

Alas, we know very well that ideals can never be completely embodied in practice. And yet, on the other hand, it is never to be forgotten that Ideals do exist; that if they be not approximated to at all, the whole matter goes to wreck!

                                      Thomas Carlyle, 150 years ago
                                              (4,999,850 HO)

Standards, Ideals, and Judgements

A most important point to be made is that animals, including the higher primates, cannot make conscious judgements because they lack the intellectual power for reference. The cow who sticks her head through the fence is attracted to the grass on the other side of the fence, but she does not consciously judge the grass as "good" or "bad" in quality. On the other hand, humans do make conscious judgements using pre-established *standards* for comparison. In the case of behavior towards others, standards can be of an ethical nature. In the case of science, the standard of reference is a comparison group with known characteristics, the *control group*.

Establishing Standards and Ideals

Because of our intellectual capacity for reference, we humans have the ability to compare differences and to consciously establish standards. The written record begins to contain examples of conscious behavioral standards several thousand years ago, although crude standards may have begun to appear before that. Examples of these early standards are religious beliefs and behaviors in the form of rites and purity codes – what to eat and what not to eat – and in secular life laws governing other types of behavior. Eventually, the human intellect conceived of theoretical standards that represented the most desirable outcome or behavior. These standards of perfection are what we call *ideals*, and they represent our highest aspirations.

Making Judgements

Thus began a type of human thinking and behavior which is completely different from that of the animals, including the higher primates, who do not have the intellectual capacity to establish standards and ideals. Having standards and ideals has led humans to another activity, consciously making judgements. In our everyday lives, we continuously make judgements about the quality of material things and about our own and other's behavior. Thus, making judgements is another unique human quality. It has been a very positive force in human affairs but, when misapplied, has also been the cause of much stress and misery. Yet, however imperfect when applied in practice, standards, ideals, and judgements are part of the essence of the human side of our nature.

External Versus Internal Standards

Without behavioral standards, life would rapidly revert to an intolerable state. We could not put up with the violence and destruction which would occur. The real question we now face is what system of standards will we use to govern our behavior. Will we continue to rely mainly on the old and imperfect animal system of applying external standards by force — law and punishment — or will we be able to more fully develop the new and uniquely human approach of applying the internal standard of Ethic to our behavior as individuals?

The Animal Nature of Humans

Man hath no better thing under the sun
than to eat and to drink and to be merry

Ecclesiastes, 2300 years ago
(4,997,700 HO)

The Animal Nature of Humans

Our Animal Needs

That humans have developed unique intellectual capacities which are not shared by any of the animals does not mean, however, that humans have also lost their basic animal nature. We still have biological needs. Four of these needs are essential to our survival as individuals — water, food, shelter from extreme cold and heat, and nurturing as infants. A fifth need, sexual reproduction, is necessary for the survival of our species. *We humans have developed our animal nature far beyond that of all other species!* What species can surpass us in such animal activities as eating, drinking, communicating, socializing, playing, having sex, parenting, building, and fighting; *all activities that do not require self-awareness*. However, having self-awareness greatly adds to the sophistication and pleasure with which we conduct these activities.

The Two Dimensions of Our Character

Thus, we retain an animal side to our nature while having gained unique human qualities. The elements which make up these two parts of our nature can be separated on the basis of whether they require only the consciousness which characterize animal existence or depend on the self-consciousness of the human intellect (Table 1).

Capacities and Characteristics

It is important to recognize that both animals and humans are capable of experiencing emotion. These *feelings* which we share, make it appear that animals are more intellectually similar to us than they really are. Animals have the capacity to feel the *simple emotions* such as love, hate, fear, happiness, and sadness which require only consciousness. We retain these emotions as part of our own animal nature.

Table 1. The Two Parts of Our Nature and Behavior

Animal (Requires consciousness)	Human (Requires self-consciousness)

Capacities
  simple emotions
  simple ideas
	Capacities
	  complex emotions
	  complex ideas

Characteristics
  acquisitiveness
  deceitfulness
  intolerance
  courage
	Characteristics
	  liberality
	  truthfulness and honesty
	  tolerance

Attitudes
  concern for self and family
  close-mindedness
  unwillingness to admit error
  unwillingness to apologize
	Attitudes
	  concern for others and strangers
	  open-mindedness
	  willingness to admit error
	  willingness to apologize

Activities
  eating
  grooming
  socializing
  displaying
  playing
  communicating
  reproducing
  parenting
  teaching, training
  tool making
  building, destroying
  assaulting
	Activities
	  establishing standards
	  making judgements
	  practicing Ethic
	  understanding principles of causality
	  practicing science

However, we have also developed other *complex emotions* such as pride, guilt, shame, and humility which require self-consciousness. Emotion is discussed in more detail later in the book. As has been discussed earlier, animals also lack the intellectual capacity for understanding complex ideas involving reference.

Animal characteristics which we retain are acquisitiveness, deceitfulness in dealing with others and intolerance of strange or different ways of appearance or behavior. An example of animal deceitfulness is the mother bird who pretends to have a broken wing in order to lure a predator from her nest. On the other hand, our human self-awareness has led to liberality and the appreciation of the value of truthfulness and honesty. It has also given us a tolerance for things that differ from us and the ways of our own species, tribes, or families. Courage is a part of our continuing animal nature, but we use it for our human purposes.

Attitudes

Our attitudes also reflect our total character, the animal and human features of our dual nature. Our animal side is reflected in our concern for ourself, our families, and friends, our close-mindedness to new ideas, and our resistance to change. Also, it is responsible for our unwillingness to admit error and to apologize – important attitudes for maintaining animal dominance which is discussed later. Our human side has led us to care for the welfare of all people, not just family and friends, to have open-mindedness to new ideas and change, and a willingness to admit error and apologize.

Activities

The two sides of our nature are also reflected in our activities. Our animal side is responsible for the activities which serve our basic needs such as eating and reproducing as well as for a wide variety of everyday activities including socializing, parenting, teaching, playing, tool making, and building. Communication – by calls, postures, and displays –

is also an animal activity, although animals do not use symbols in communication as we do. Finally, the animal side of our nature leads to the destructive behavior we exhibit in assaulting and killing others and in destroying. All of these types of behavior are carried out routinely by lower animals, clearly showing that such activities do not require self-awareness.

The types of activities requiring self-awareness and associated with the human side of our nature are more limited. These include consciously setting internal and external standards, making judgements relative to these standards, practicing Ethic, understanding the principles of causality, and practicing science. In the same way that emotions and ideas have been classified, as simple and complex, it is possible to categorize our animal activities as *simple activities* and our human activities as *complex activities* since they depend on different levels of intellectual capacity.

Emotion

The Furies have me now,
they burn, they drive!

Virgil, 2000 years ago
(4,998,000 HO)

Emotion

Emotion Part of Animal Nature

We are conscious of our emotions, but it is important to realize that experiencing an emotion is not the same as having a thought – *feeling an emotion is not an intellectual activity.* Children less than a year old are able to experience what are termed "primary" emotions such as joy, sadness, fear, and anger. However, it is not until children are close to three years old and have developed self-consciousness that they are able to acquire the more complicated emotions such as embarrassment, shame, and empathy. These emotions are dependent on self-awareness. Animals share the same primary emotions with humans. It is obvious that emotion arose as part of our animal nature.

Biologic Basis for Emotion

Next to our biological needs for survival, emotion is our most common and powerful stimulus for action. Animals and humans behave in similar ways when under similar emotional states. Thus, we see that anger leads to fighting, joy leads to celebration, and fear leads to flight. Emotion and the behavior associated with emotion are "hardwired." This means that there is a direct biological connection between an emotion and its associated behavior which is mediated by chemical and nerve pathways. This connection results in a predictable response when the emotion is elicited. It does not require thinking – use of intellect. In fact, it often happens before there is time to think. When somebody "yanks your chain," they are taking advantage of this hardwired connection between emotion and response. If you have a "short fuse" – a strong connection – it does not take long for you to respond.

The behavioral response to a primary emotion is thought to be less restrained in animals than in humans, but everyday experience shows that there are many exceptions to this generality. Some humans respond with uncontrollable, homicidal rage to minor provocations, manslaughter provoked by a minor traffic accident, being an example. And animals sometimes seem to show admirable restraint when provoked past the point that an aggressive response would be warranted.

However, in general, to the extent that the conscience is working, the human, on average, appears to show better control of emotional behavior than the animal. The degree to which this is true has not been well studied, if studied at all, and it would be interesting to compare rates of emotional response in humans and animals under similar conditions of provocation. The provocation would have to be done by members of the same species. It would not be fair to have hungry foxes provoked by tender rabbits.

Complex Human Emotions

We must deal not only with our destructive animal emotions such as anger when frustrated, but also with the complex emotions which have developed along with self-awareness. It has been proposed that the strongest and most painful of these emotions is shame. Michael Lewis has written most persuasively of feeling the powerful results of shame and its importance in causing paralysis of the intellect and anger, both at oneself and at others. Shame is such a powerful, painful, and paralyzing emotion that often we appear to be unaware of its presence. Because of the pain and discomfort that shame can elicit, it is not allowed to reach or remain at a conscious level. This makes shame an especially difficult emotion for us to manage.

Shame

Shame is defined by Michael Lewis as an emotion in which the focus is solely on self in distinction to guilt where the focus is on an external event. An example is the situation of a child breaking a toy. With shame, the child's focus is inward on his or her own inadequacy and behavior is inhibited and confused, leading to inaction. With guilt, the focus is outward, leading to attempts to mend the toy and confessions to other people. Shame is associated with damage to our self-image from perceived lapses in adherence to our personal values and standards. Because of differences in these personal values, one individual may shame another without being aware of having done it. Shame represents a particularly violent collision between the vanity which supports our feeling of self-worth and the intellectual self-recognition that we have failed ourselves. Shame results from the recognition that we are not so "human" after all, that we are acting like an animal. That for various reasons — lack of "human" character, lack of "human" talent, "animal" laziness, "animal" hunger — we have behaved in a way that is unbecoming to ourselves as a "human being."

We also recognize that persons who are incapable of feeling shame find it difficult, if not impossible, to refrain from animal behavior, to behave like humans. We recognize this when we characterize especially destructive behavior as "shameless". Thus, on an emotional level, *possessing shame is a defining human characteristic.*

Personal Standards and Shame

We fail ourselves from time to time if we try to accomplish anything. Karen Blixen, better known by the name she used as an author, Isak Dinesen, wrote "He who makes no mistakes seldom makes anything." What is most under our control in determining if and when we will fail and experience shame is the content of our own personal standard. If the feature of most importance in our standard relates to an animal quest for dominance — "keeping up with or bettering the Joneses" — we will be concerned with things such as being the best dressed, the most clever, the best spoken, the richest, and the most powerful. This standard makes us susceptible to events beyond our control. If our child performs poorly in a piano recital, if we fail to get a promotion, or if someone ridicules our new clothes, we will feel shame. If, on the other hand, the most important feature of our personal standard relates to our own behavior in leading our lives in an ethical way, we will still fail ourselves from time to time and feel shame, but now the matter is under our own control. The shame we feel when we fail ourselves is for a worthy human purpose and not related to animalistic material goals.

Balance Between Emotional Behavior and Ethical Control

In this setting of hardwired and potentially destructive emotional response, we, of all living creatures, are in a unique position because of our conscience. We alone have developed a self-judgmental control mechanism for regulating emotional behavior. *The balance between emotional stimulation of destructive behavior – our animal heritage – and ethical control of such behavior – our human development – is the most important dynamic of human affairs.* Unfortunately, there is frequently imbalance in the wrong direction – our emotions rule.

Controlling Emotional Behavior

The desired balance can be achieved by 1) suppressing destructive behavior by external restraint and punishment, 2) strengthening the internal ethical control of such behavior, and 3) lessening the opportunities for events leading to emotions such as anger and shame.

Punishment, restraint, and an emphasis on ethical conduct have been tried the longest with some apparent success. But without being able to observe another world in which these measures were not taken – a "control group" – we can never know for sure how successful they have been. In more recent times, greater emphasis has been placed on the approach of lessening human anger and frustration by improving material well-being. The same problem exists in evaluating the success of this approach, no control group exists for comparison.

What is abundantly clear is that none of these approaches has eliminated violent behavior associated with our primary needs and emotions, and a spirited dialogue continues among supporters of the different approaches. We like to believe that for whatever reason the level of human violence has declined over the ages, but there is little if any solid support for this view. Our own century has established the record for the highest absolute number of victims of human violence, although, of course, world populations are also larger than in the past.

It appears unlikely that our capacity for strong emotional feelings and destructive behavior, because of their biologic basis, will change anytime soon. It is possible that genetic engineering could conceivably alter our capacity for destructive emotional responses. Because we humans do not trust ourselves to behave ethically, eugenics – human genetic engineering – is currently not considered an acceptable practice for altering behavior. Also, the idea of eugenics threatens a more basic fear we have, the loss of individual free will. However, were we ever to adopt the use of genetic alteration to control behavior, having an ethical standard as the basis of our conduct would become all the more important.

For the foreseeable future, we will continue to face this great behavioral challenge as we exist today. For now, we must accept that emotion, often strongly felt, is part of our normal animal being, and we must learn to control it better. As a species, we have developed a unique and effective mechanism for emotional control, the conscience. Also, with our skills and intellect, we can continue to improve material conditions and thus possibly reduce conditions which provoke frustration and anger.

However, we should recognize that the historical record shows that material conditions are immeasurably better now than in the past and that wholesale violence is still with us. Also, for the present, we can not forsake humane punishments and restraints when they are needed to protect us from individuals lacking self-control. Abundant experimental evidence shows that punishment – negative reinforcement – suppresses unwanted behavior in animals, and, based on experience, we know it does the same for people who show animal behavior. However, it is not a perfect solution, and to be effective, negative reinforcement requires frequent repetition or its effect decays. This presents a problem in effectively applying it to human behavior.

The Positive Interaction
of Intellect and Emotion

We know the truth, not only by
the reason, but by the heart

                        Blaise Pascal, 350 years ago
                               (4,999,650 HO)

The Positive Interaction of Intellect and Emotion

To reach our full *human* potential, we have to understand ourselves. We have to understand how we function. We have to understand how our "parts" work. And the two parts which we must understand the best are our human intellect and our animal emotion. What is written in the previous chapter gives the impression that the intellect and the emotion function independently, and that the two are usually in conflict. While this is true in many circumstances, it is also important to recognized that *intellect and emotion also undergo a critical positive interaction*, and that it is this interaction which really governs how we ultimately think and act. When our intellect and our emotions are in "sync," we listen! We believe! We act!

Emotion Is Required for Acceptance of Ideas

Put simply, unless our ideas have an emotional connection, they have no power to influence our beliefs or behavior. We are "seeing" but not believing. "Our hearts are not in it." We recognize the truth, the logic of the idea, but do not incorporate it into our personal "beliefs," and so it does not govern our thinking and behavior. Our strong personal beliefs are ideas that carry an emotional charge — "fighting words," "gut feelings," "sincere beliefs," "hopes and fears."

Lack of Positive Emotional Response to New Information about Our Nature

In our current stage of development as a species, our intellects are discovering remarkable new facts about ourselves which are discussed in this book. This information is brand new and as such, it interests us. We read the new information about ourselves in newspapers and magazines, we see it on television. It tickles our intellect — "my, that is interesting" — but our emotions do not connect to it in a positive way. Therefore, it has not become a part of us. The new ideas are connected to no emotion except perhaps fear. We forget the new ideas when we put down the magazine which contain them or when the television program describing these things is over. They do not influence our behavior. They are not part of us when we go to bed at night and when we get up in the morning. We do not take them to work with us. We have not emotionalized the fact that our ancestors originated five million years ago as animals and that our own animal nature is still present and overpowering. *We have not emotionalized the fact that if we do not practice Ethic, we are animals.* Are we capable of giving this idea a positive emotional charge? Can it make us feel good?

The Human Nature of Humans

Time Lines of When the Animal and Human Features of Our Intellect Appeared

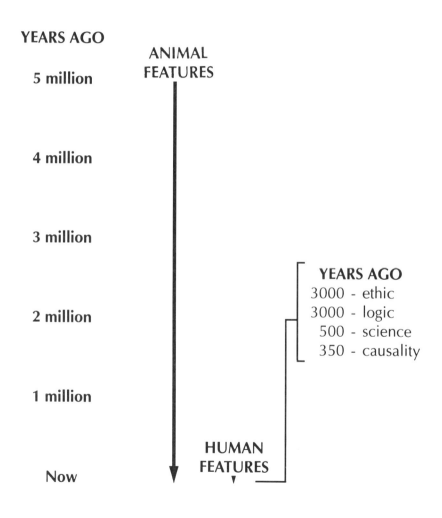

The Human Nature of Humans

If a wide range of our day-to-day activities and emotions are part of our continuing animal nature, what uniquely *human* features can be recognized in our behavior? What thoughts and actions derive from the capacity of our intellect which separate us from the animals? How often are these strictly human thoughts and actions displayed in everyday life? In your own everyday life, how often do you behave like a "human" human instead of an "animal" human?

Self-Analysis Allows Ethical Behavior

Self-analysis of behavior is the most important non-animal capability which humans possess. The appearance of self-critical thinking produced a concern for telling the truth, not stealing, and caring for others. As this ethical maxim has been expanded, it has been applied to many aspects of behavior between individuals or groups. Such specific behaviors as telling the truth about items for sale, not cheating on examinations, not assaulting others, and providing care for persons in need are commonplace examples.

Human Understanding of Causation

Humans have also developed the intellectual capacity to consciously understand causation of natural events. This capability is also based on self-awareness, having a sense of "reference," and the ability to make judgements. Understanding causation not only requires self-awareness but also having a greater intellectual capacity than that of the higher primates. Understanding causation has led to our ability to practice science. It is important not to confuse making tools, an animal activity, with practicing science, a uniquely human activity. Tool making by animals may involve a certain amount of instinctive trial and error but it does not require the intellectual capacity to practice science. Tool making can be done without conscious experimentation and an understanding of the principles of causality.

Our Human Qualities Have Just Appeared

Although *our genetic line started to separate from the lines of the higher primates some five million years ago*, the written record of human history only began approximately six thousand years ago. *Our concern with ethical behavior, as expressed in the written record, began not much earlier than three thousand years ago as did a beginning understanding of causality.* The practice of science based on more sophisticated understanding of causality developed over the past five hundred years.

If you take the approximately 5000 years that it is reasonable to believe we have shown distinct human thought — as defined by the conscious understanding of ethical behavior and causality — and divide it by the five million years we have been evolving as a separate species, you arrive at 0.1%. *Only 0.1% — one one-thousandths — of the entire period of our existence have we been truly human.* Put another way, we have lived as animals — without ethical behavior or an understanding of causality — for 99.9% of the period we have been evolving as a species. Even if the more unlikely period of 50,000 years is selected as when the human intellect first consciously conceived of the idea of Ethic and began to understand causality, it still represents only 1% of the time we have been developing as a species. It is not surprising that our human side has a tenuous hold on our animal behavior.

Burial of the dead, which was increasingly accompanied by ritual, became a regular feature of our culture in the Upper Paleolithic period, which began approximately 50 thousand years ago. The presence of grave goods in burial sites suggests that belief in an afterlife may have appeared, indicating that we were acquiring an understanding of the significance of death and possibly beginning to practice religion. However, the nature of primitive religion, which included human sacrifice and ritual cannibalism, is more animalistic than human in its features. Religious beliefs, associated with a true human standard, appeared only within the past few thousand years, associated with the expressed conscious understanding of the principle of Ethic.

Henry David Thoreau, in considering the mystery of human origins, described the usual *feelings* we have about time and our human existence as follows: "three thousand years deep into time...can you well go further back in history than this?" We consider a few thousand years as going back to our real beginnings. As part of the creation myth of our tribal origins, we have narrowly limited the time span over which we see ourselves as existing on the earth. In the Judeo-Christian version of the myth, we descend from Adam and Eve to the time of Christ in sixty odd generations – sixty some generations, approximately 6000 years (early biblical life spans averaged 900 years). *This is very different from the five million-year time span over which we have actually evolved as a species.* Five million years of biologic need and emotion. Five million years without self-awareness and self-judgement. Five million years without Ethic. Five million years without intellectual understanding of causality. Five million years in animal darkness. Five million years determines our nature. Five million years is so deep into our past that it makes it very hard – if not impossible – for us to be emotionally able to accept that it was five million years.

Ontogeny Recapitulates Phylogeny

Of course, our real origin goes back much further than five million years. Our real origin goes back to the beginning of life on earth, some four billion years ago. In biology, ontogeny recapitulates phylogeny. What that means in plain language is that the embryonic development of each individual animal reflects the developmental history of the species to which that animal belongs. For us, that means that during our embryonic development, while developing in our mother's womb, we each go through a temporary stage in which we have gills like a fish and a tail like an animal. These parts disappear as we develop to full maturity as an unborn baby, but during our formative development before birth, we reflect the distant evolutionary history of our species.

Human Behavior Absent at Birth

Unlike our physical form, which has become fully human at birth, our thought and behavior at birth retain their animal character. We are born little animals – without self-awareness and without a conscience – and we retain an animal side to our nature throughout life. Later, through intellectual maturation, we develop the capacity for self-awareness and self-judgement, the things that make us human. This, however, is not to say that infants and young children should not be cherished and loved as humans or that the sanctity of their lives be less respected than that of adults.

Ethic

Do not do to others what you do
not want them to do to you.

Confucius, 2500 years ago
(4,997,500 HO)

Ethic

Terminology

The term "ethics" is the cause of serious and harmful confusion. There is only *one* human ethic. Stated more accurately, *there is only one "Ethic."* Ethic is a uniquely human intellectual concept which cannot be accurately applied in any other than a human context. Ethic needs no qualification as being "human." The concept of animal ethic is an absurdity. Animals lack the intellectual capacity for self-judgement and, therefore, do not have the ability to understand or practice Ethic.

Origin of Ethic

When the human intellect conceived of the concept of Ethic, a surpassing new way of thinking appeared, and the world has never been the same. Exactly when the idea appeared will never be known and is unimportant. What is important is to appreciate that this idea appeared only after millions of years of the development of our species had occurred and that it is associated with our unique intellectual capacity for self-judgement. Without the capacity for self-judgement and the ability to create ideals of personal behavior, it would not be possible to understand the concept of Ethic. While altruistic behavior – actions which may benefit others – must have developed over time as an earlier feature of our nature, its self-conscious awareness and its expression as a desirable personal standard appear to have occurred recently as a rather sudden event. Ethic could only have been consciously conceived of and expressed during the period between 50,000 and 5000 years ago. More likely it was closer to 5000 than 50,000 years ago. The reason for believing in the latter date is that the earliest religious and philosophic writings do not mention the ideal. It does not appear in the written record until approximately 2500 years ago. In the *Analects*, when asked what was the *one* guiding principle,

Confucius said "Do not do to others what you do not want them to do to you." In *Leviticus*, it is written that Moses said "Love thy neighbor as thyself." In the *Dhammapada*, Buddha said "Consider others as yourself." And in *Luke*, Jesus said "Do unto others as you would have them do unto you."

Definition of Ethic

What is Ethic? A secular version of Ethic is **to care about others in the truthful and honest way in which you would wish others to care about you.**

A sacred version of Ethic is **to love others in the truthful and honest way in which you would wish others to love you; and to love your God**.

And what is the practice of Ethic? **The practice of Ethic is to apply this principle to everything in your life, everyday of your life**.

Does an Understanding of Ethic Appear in All People

A most important question is whether all people develop the intellectual capacity for Ethic or is this something that spontaneously arises in only some people and is learned – or not – by others. No one has done the experiment – nor should they – of raising a group of children from birth in an environment which is devoid of all human intellectual content to determine if any, some, or all will develop a conscience. In the 13th century, King Frederick II of Sicily actually did try to raise infants under such conditions to determine what language they would speak after having had no human intellectual contact. The children all died from the failure to thrive that affects infants who do not receive sufficient human contact and nurturing. But the important question of do all people develop the intellectual capacity to understand the principle of Ethic remains unanswered. This obviously has enormous practical implications for what we teach children.

Misuse of Terminology

The term "ethical" is commonly misused to mean "fair." As in "Are differences in breast cancer screening rates by race ethical?" Such questions are raised and debated by well meaning individuals and groups who then try to apply a standard for influencing the behavior of *other people*. This is not an activity that originates from within the individual, as does Ethic.

In this usage, the term "ethics" is used to describe an intellectual discipline involving the development and application of behavioral standards to social issues. Should abortion be allowed? Is euthanasia legal? These are questions for which there is no way to determine scientific truth, as discussed in the next chapter. They can only be decided by the *emotional feelings* of the majority, in which case the feelings of the minority may be ignored.

For an individual or a group to develop behavioral standards – even after sincere and serious study – and to try to impose or force these standards on others is a form of animal – not human – behavior. It is animal behavior because it involves modifying the behavior of others – training – not modifying the behavior of one's own self – Ethic. In our current stage of development this may be necessary at times, but from a *human* perspective, it is undesirable and distasteful and should be used only as a last resort in serious matters. Also, it can lead to harmful self-delusion if a person practicing the activity believes that it bestows on him or her "ethical" superiority.

In addition, there is the danger that this practice of "ethics" can be abused for philosophical and political reasons. There is the greater danger that it can be used as a convenient way to avoid facing the true meaning of *Ethic* and its practice in our own personal lives. Groups such as "ethics committees" create the risk that we as individuals will rely on the judgement of others and thus avoid facing our own Ethical responsibility. Also, if we do not like the opinions of such groups, we may be able to change or, in the final analysis, ignore them. After all, we may reason, these are only decisions made by a group of fallible people. And, of course, most people don't have access to ethics committees to guide their actions. If we attempted to supply everyone with this service, a major shortage of "ethicists" would very soon occur. And, to repeat, what happens to individual conscience in the process? This is not to say that many well-meaning people have not taught "ethics," worked on "ethics committees," and in other ways sincerely tried to improve human behavior. But it does emphasize that the study of "ethics" and *the imposition of "ethical standards" on other people is a very different thing from the practice of Ethic by each individual.*

The Uncomplicated Nature of Ethic

In reality, the concept of Ethic and its practice is patently obvious and ridiculously simple to people who have the intellectual capacity to understand it. *Would we want this to happen to us?* This is the standard. It does not require any interpretation. Once the concept is understood, self-judgement supplies the standard. An expert is not needed to explain the meaning of Ethic or to instruct its practice. Ethic is not subject to coercion. It cannot be forced on anyone, although it may possibly be elicited in children as they mature by teaching and example. *Ethic belongs to each one of us who has the intellectual development to have a conscience.* Imposing a set of "ethics" on someone without a conscience is an impossibility. As discussed above, that type of approach is really a form of animal training.

Ethic Unifies All Humans

Despite the current diversity of philosophic and religious beliefs — which may be more apparent than real — in what has been called the "post-modern" age, there *is* one unifying *human* worldview. *The* human worldview is Ethic; it transcends all diversity — sexual, ethnic, geographic, cultural, philosophic, and religious. Ethic is *the* unifying human worldview because it applies the same self-defining standard to each of us. Are you animal or are you human? *You, through your every day thinking and behavior, define yourself.* And this defining is based not on philosophical theory but on the biological reality of the difference in behavior between animals and humans. Ethic is the worldview that unites all *humans*, because without it, you simply are not human.

Workings of Ethic

Do unto others as you would have them do unto you

Jesus, 2000 years ago
(4,998,000 HO)

Workings of Ethic

Ethic is a Principle

Ethic is in the category of a *principle* or *law* which deals with caring about others. As a principle, it is important to know, if possible, if Ethic operates as a law of natural biologic behavior or as a principle of human free-will based on philosophic theory and belief. This will be discussed later in relation to the question of the existence of human free-will. For the time being, the discussion will focus on issues related to the function of Ethic.

Does Ethic Work

For the present, assuming that Ethic has reality, the first question will be "Does the practice of Ethic really work"? Does the practice of Ethic result in measurable changes in behavior, and are these changes constructive? To answer these questions, it must be possible to define and measure behavioral change and to define and measure what is "constructive". At this point, it should be pointed out that such an experiment has never been done in the history of the world. No one has ever taken a group composed of persons who practice Ethic and prospectively compared them to an otherwise similar group of persons who do not practice Ethic for such things as murder rates, assault rates, rates of stealing, or defined "quality of life" rates in the respective groups. All the information we have to address this question relies on comparisons using what are called historical controls. Do individuals or groups who have adopted the behavioral standard of Ethic show less murderous and assaultive behavior, steal less, and in other ways show more respect for other people then before they adopted the ethical behavior? The historical record suggests that this is true as well as the testimonials of persons who have undergone such a change. That is all that can be said in answer to the question.

Application of Ethic in Real Life

A second important question is whether Ethic can be applied broadly to human interactive behavior. It seems reasonable to conclude – unless convoluted and absurd reasoning is used – that all normal persons would not like to be murdered – as opposed to killed in warfare, which might be viewed differently. Therefore, dislike of being murdered can be considered as a consistent personal value of normal persons. Thus, persons practicing the principle of Ethic, and having this value, would be expected to not murder other people. Other similar and obvious examples of uniform personal values can be thought of such as dislike of being assaulted, dislike of being robbed, and dislike of being cheated.

What about lying? Lying is often used for dishonest ends and as such is ethically undesirable. What is more important is *that to lie to someone is a sign of disrespect for that person*. With a lie, you are trying to "fool" someone. This shows that you consider them capable of being fooled – of being a fool – an indication of serious lack of respect. People who understand this do not want to be lied to because they know it is disrespectful. In this important way, lying violates Ethic.

But situations can be imagined involving telling the truth in which personal values may differ from person-to-person. An example frequently used is the question of whether to honestly inform the dying person that he or she is dying. One person's personal values on this question may be to want to know the truth while another's may be to want to avoid knowing the truth. How does one practice Ethic in this situation? Does the ethical person who personally desires to have the knowledge of imminent death tell other persons of the fact since that is what they themselves would have wanted? And does the ethical person who does not want to be informed of imminent death withhold this information from others because of their own personal value? This obviously presents a problem. Does this kind of problem diminish the practical value of Ethic as the standard of human behavior? The answer is no. While there are differences in individual personal values, as a rule *normal persons do not want to experience physical or emotional pain which is needless or not of their own choosing.* Therefore, Ethic teaches that they should not want to impose such pain on others. This *universal personal standard* makes it possible to successfully circumvent the problem of differing personal values on specific issues and to use Ethic to deal with most situations which arise in interactions between mentally competent adults. This requires making an effort to understand a person's personal values and standards before taking action in potentially hurtful situations which involve them. Thus, for example, the individual who declares or indirectly indicates that they do not wish to know about impending death can be treated differently from the individual who does, and, thus, maintain the universal standard of avoiding causing pain. But remember, these situations are unusual and *most lying is an attempt to benefit the liar, not to benefit the person to whom the lie is told*. Other aspects of lying are discussed later in the section on ways in which the intellect is misled.

Of course, there will always be mistakes and various practical problems with the practice of Ethic just as there are in any other human activity. Adopting the practice of Ethic does not guarantee that you will achieve perfection! Do not expect that. And adopting this ideal and practice does not mean supporting the self-destructive or destructive behavior of persons of questionable intellectual competence. Most importantly, we must not take the attitude that because the practice of Ethic can never be perfect it is not worth trying. The intellectual trap of utopian thinking is discussed later in this book. It is a bad one! Experience suggests that even flawed attempts to practice Ethic are much better than no attempt at all.

Ethic and Children

Another question is how does Ethic apply to children? We have already seen that young children do not have the intellectual capacity for self-awareness and self-judgement. Therefore, they, like animals, are unable to practice Ethic.

This is a biological reality. But what about the behavior of adults towards children? With the young child in whom reason is not effective in preventing self-destructive or destructive behavior, restraints which may cause physical or emotional distress are required to prevent the child from engaging in such behavior. They are obviously necessary. Young children cannot be allowed to play with fire! What about the older child or the "childish" adult? Again, destructive or self-destructive behavior cannot be allowed even if associated with distress for the individual. But we must be humane and reasonable in these situations. Do what we believe is best for the individual, not for ourselves. And try to know when they have become "adult," – that is human – when they have developed intellects which are capable of practicing Ethic. Then their behavior may "improve" because they do not want to give *us* pain. What a wonderful day!

Components of Ethic

And finally, how does Ethic work at a functional level? What are its components? Ethic is an intellectual understanding of a sophisticated *human* idea which is dependent on the capacity for self-judgement. But the value judgements in Ethic are directed by emotional feelings. Thus, the concept of *reciprocity* – treating others as you would wish to be treated – is intellectual. The content – the way you wish to be treated in a specific situation – is based on your emotional reaction to that situation. The dynamic of Ethic employs both our human intellectual understanding and our animal emotions.

Emotion and Ethical Behavior

Emotion is a much, much stronger force in our lives than intellect. Emotion has been with us from the beginning. Emotion is in part responsible for Ethic. Both altruistic and selfish motives are involved in the practice of Ethic. The altruistic part is concern and love – concern and love for others. But also, we ourselves do not want to be hurt so we avoid hurting others in hope that they will avoid *hurting* us. Not only our emotional feelings, but also the intellectual concept of justice contributes to Ethic. In this way, Ethic is related to fairness, *fairness as judged by each individual conscience.*

Being human, requires using our intellectual capacity to control destructive emotions. But if we reduce emotion excessively, we become "hard," we become "calculating," we become "machines," we may become "unloved" by others. Many people are so threatened by the prospect of being unloved that they neglect their intellect and give their emotions free rein, thus, becoming poor parents or unethical in their dealing with others. Ethical behavior may be very hard or even impossible for people who so fear being unloving that they are paralyzed by emotion. But, being too rational is also a danger. Excessive rationality in the absence of positive emotional feelings has led to horrible things in our history. The concept of "breaking some eggs" – the cold blooded destroying of people – to gain a "rational" philosophic or political goal has led to large scale brutality and murder. It is a danger which can only be avoided by binding our emotion and our intellect to the principle of Ethic. *Ethic is the one intellectual standard to which we can safely commit our emotion.* With Ethic, we have our most reliable principle for relating to others. With Ethic we can control the awesome power of the other product of our human intellect, science. With Ethic as our standard, we can use our intellect to its fullest and still be emotional and loving individuals.

Loving Message of the Book

An idea requires an emotional connection to become established as a belief. As discussed later, emotion is often produced by *external* forces which affect our lives – fear of danger, privation and hunger, love received. This book is written in the hope that it will strike a responsive chord in your heart. This book is written as a message of friendship and love. I hope you will accept it as such. Then its message will become a part of you.

Causality

Is probability probable?

Blaise Pascal, 350 years ago
(4,999,650 HO)

P = < 0.01

Causality

Sensory Perception

Humans have recently gone through several stages in attempting to understand the cause of natural events. In the beginning and for a very long time, our unconscious animal stage of understanding depended entirely on the perception of our senses, as it still does with animals. Even today, sensory perception remains a major force in shaping our ideas of causation, "seeing is believing."

Supernatural Force

Beginning approximately 50,000 years ago, we began to exhibit behavior, such as ritual burial, which suggested that the intellect had conceived of the concept of supernatural power. From this way of thinking arose the idea that natural events were associated with the will of supernatural powers present in celestial and natural objects with which our early ancestors were familiar (Table 2). This belief – the will of the gods – eventually evolved into the religions which exist today, which in most cases are now based on belief in one Supreme Deity. Inherent in contemporary religious thinking is the concept of the Deity as the *first cause* of all events regardless of their causal explanation on a more superficial level.

It has taken our intellect a very long time – on the scale of written history – to advance beyond the concepts of sensory perception and supernatural power as the only understandable idea in the area of causality. Superstitious rites and the worship of multiple deities continued on a large scale until very recent times and exist today in some cultures. Intellects capable of building remarkable early civilizations in the Middle East and Asia down to the early European Classical Period continued to interpret causation through the experience of the senses – what we call "common sense" – and through mythical supernatural forces, "the gods." Superstition remains a powerful force in human thinking even now.

Table 2. Stages of Human Understanding of Causation

Stage	Type of Understanding	Content
I	Superstition	Belief that natural events are controlled by supernatural power
II	Logic	Understanding that the cause of natural events can be determined by the intellect
III	Science	Understanding that natural events can be simulated and their cause determined by comparative testing
IV	Quality control of science	Understanding that the quality of science can be improved by controlling for chance and bias

The Understanding of Logic

The next step in human understanding of causation, the intellectual concept of *logic*, appeared only approximately 3000 years ago. With the appearance of logic, the human intellect had consciously conceived of a radically new idea. This idea was that the human intellect itself did not need direct divine assistance to be superior to the perception of the senses in understanding causation. It was consciously recognized that "looks can be deceiving" and that observations of events when placed in a logical framework could lead to truth. William Budd — the man who discovered how typhoid fever spreads — described the fallibility of the senses when he said "Nature does not wear her heart on her sleeve."

Logic became an important part of our thinking, and it continues to play an essential role in human intellectual understanding of causation. However, even today, logic's hold on the everyday thinking and behavior of each of us remains fragile. We routinely allow our thinking to be governed by sensory perception, superstition, and emotion. When we think about it, this is all too obvious. Frederick the Great observed that "We are governed by passion and very rarely by reason."

The fragility of logical thinking is not surprising considering the millions of years our species existed before we discovered logic and the very brief period in which our intellect has been capable of using logical thinking in understanding causation.

The Understanding of Science

Logic arose as a new and powerful way to understand the cause of natural events. It immediately began to yield important new knowledge. Logic produced the framework for the academic disciplines which have increased human knowledge immensely in recent centuries. But waiting for interesting natural events to occur was slow and limited the rate at which new knowledge could be acquired. The human intellect responded with another remarkable advance which was the next stage in understanding causation, experimental science. If observing natural events is a slow process, then why not deliberately manipulate nature and observe what happens? To benefit the most from this new activity, it was necessary to observe the difference between the manipulated state and the state when nature is not manipulated. This is formal comparative testing, which is the definition of *science*. Science has turned out to be the most powerful, exciting, and frightening achievement of our intellect – at least in relation to material things. Science has given us the power to change the world – which we have rapidly done – and the power to destroy the world – which so far, we have not done. Science has now given us the power to change life itself, through manipulation of the genetic code. In a material – as opposed to spiritual – sense we now understand causation in a detail previously unimaginable.

Science and Mathematics

In addition to manipulating nature itself, we have learned how to use mathematical symbols which represent elements of nature. We then manipulate these symbols to acquire new information. This information becomes knowledge when we subsequently observe or manipulate nature itself and confirm the mathematical findings. For example, Albert Einstein's mathematical theory of relativity was confirmed by the experiments in physics which produced nuclear fission.

Science and Prediction

Thus, an important part of science, in addition to testing, is predicting. What has been learned through scientific experimentation – new information – should apply not only to the experimental condition that produced the information but also to that condition when it is encountered in the real world. This transforms *information* into *knowledge*. If this does not happen, if the new information cannot be generalized, then there may be something wrong with the new information, it may not be correct.

Quality Control of Science

It is now recognized that scientific experimentation, just like any other human activity, is subject to errors and mistakes. An important test of this possibility is to use the new information to make predictions about what will happen in the future. By this approach, it has been possible to learn what causes inaccurate results in scientific research. This has led to a human understanding of causality at an even more sophisticated level. This latest intellectual advance has provided the insight that the quality of science can be measured and, thus, controlled. It is now recognized that two – and only two – extraneous forces affect the outcome of honest scientific experimentation. These are *chance* and *bias*. Chance and bias can never be eliminated from a scientific experiment – or from life itself – but they can be controlled by experimental design.

Evaluating the Role of Chance

The possibility of chance affecting a scientific experiment can be measured by appropriate statistical analysis. This is done by measuring the *probability* of chance affecting experimental results – determining the "P" (probability) value. *The symbol P <0.01, which introduces this chapter, means that there is less than a 1 in 100 probability of an observed result being due to chance alone and not because of the effect being measured.* The Theory of Probability was the product of the brilliant intellects of Blaise Pascal and his collaborator, Pierre Fermet. This is one of the great discoveries in human knowledge. It was made only 350 years ago.

Why This Understanding Is Important

If you do not apply your own intellect to understanding why things happen, you are not fulfilling your human potential. We often do not. It has been observed that to most people nothing is more troublesome than the effort of thinking. Oh, we usually have an opinion – "our opinion" – But is it really *our* opinion? That remarkable intellect, Leonardo da Vinci supplied the answer to that question when he wrote "whoever in discussion adduces authority uses not intellect by memory." In other words "our opinion" is often only what we remember to think, based on what we were told to think by a television commentator, newspaper editor, or friend – or unsuspected enemy. It is not our own opinion at all. We never even tried to use our own intellect, and yet it awaits for our use like some marvelous new machine which has never been removed from its packing box.

We should understand the principles of causality, first of all, because it is exciting and fulfilling. Leonardo da Vinci who certainly knew the feeling, spoke of "intellectual passion." Socrates believed that "The life which is unexamined is not worth living." Also, on a more practical level, it is greatly to our benefit. There are many people who will use our lack of understanding of causality in ways that are harmful to us. We are the subject of both accidental and calculated misuse of "scientific" information everyday. Scientific knowledge from the field of psychology is used to manipulate our emotions, leading us to purchase unwanted or inferior products, get us to use ineffective medical treatments, plant self-serving political ideas in our heads, and give us emotions which obstruct the administration of justice. Phoney "scientific" information and inaccurate "statistics" are used to do the same things. Without being armed with an understanding of causality, we are vulnerable to these assaults. We will be "taken" and what's worse, we may not even realize that we have been "taken." Also, more importantly, without an understanding of causation, it is difficult to make sound judgements on which to base our own ethical behavior.

Understanding causality and how to recognize and handle the effects of chance and bias on our thinking is beyond the scope of this book. However, the principles for doing this are not difficult to understand when explained properly. This is something everyone should understand. Ask someone who knows. If you are a student, ask your teachers.

Testability Defines Science and Excludes Religion and Philosophy

And finally, it is very important to understand that *causation can only be determined in matters that are testable*. Testability defines science. Untestable questions for which we can only express our feelings – value judgements – fall into the categories of philosophy and religion. These are important matters but they fall in the realm of faith, not science. Faith will be discussed later in the book.

Difficulties of the Theory

Long before the reader has arrived at this part of the work, a crowd of difficulties will have occurred to him.

Charles Darwin, 150 years ago
(4,999,850 HO)

Difficulties of the Theory

In the present work, many difficulties will also have occurred to the reader. Some of these difficulties may only be apparent, and others that are real may not bear directly on the essential ideas and, thus, may not be fatal to the theory. The difficulties may be classified under the following headings: First, what is the evidence that humans are in large part animal and not a totally unique and different form of life? Secondly, how do we know that humans and higher primates have self-consciousness while other animals do not? Thirdly, is there evidence that animals do not have the intellectual capacity for reference? Fourthly, is it possible that human intellect has a qualitative capacity not shared by any of the animals? Finally, how to address the question, "Do humans actually have free will which allows them to practice Ethic?" These questions will be discussed separately.

On the Animal Nature of Humans

The question of the animal nature of humans can be approached at several different levels: structural, functional, behavioral, chemical, and archaeological. There is very powerful evidence that humans show strong affinity to animals at all of these levels. On the structural level, human organs are fundamentally the same as the organs of most higher animals. Thus, both humans and animals have brains, nerves, muscles, lungs, livers, guts, kidneys, reproductive, and other organs, all of which need not be elaborated to make the point. Animal and human organs also look similar so that it is possible to recognize a heart from its appearance whether it comes from a cat, a deer, a pigeon, or a human. Furthermore, the function of these organs is the same in humans and animals, thus, a heart pumps blood, a lung transfers certain gases from the air into the blood and back, a gut absorbs nutrients from food which is eaten, and a kidney excretes liquid wastes, to give some obvious examples.

At a behavioral level, and despite many idiosyncratic differences among the species, there are unifying, social behaviors which are basic to humans and many animals. One such behavior is *the striving for dominance among peers*. The similarities between human and chimpanzee dominance-seeking behavior is unmistakable. The characteristics of real life human striving for dominance will be described in the discussion of bureaucracy. When shorn of the cultural devices which adorn our behavior and viewed without our accustomed vanity, dominance seeking in humans cannot help but be recognized as exactly the same behavior that is seen in many species of animals.

The newest and strongest evidence of the animal nature of humans is provided by the chemical comparisons of human and higher primate DNA. To understand and *believe* this evidence, it is necessary to understand DNA. DNA is nothing more than *information* in the form of a chemical code which is stored in the genes. The amount of information in DNA is so enormous that it is somewhat difficult to comprehend. Nevertheless, DNA is still nothing more than information – information which contains a message. The message contained in DNA is the instructions on how to build a living thing. Chimpanzee DNA has information which tells how to build a chimpanzee. Human DNA has information which tells how to build a human. Chemical testing shows that the DNA of human and chimpanzee genes is 99% the same. Knowing this fact, one may ask, "How can the DNAs be so very similar and yet humans and chimpanzees be so very different?" The answer to that is in the very large amount of information which is contained in primate DNA. The amount is so huge that 1% still allows for a large amount of information to be different in human and chimpanzee DNA. So, you may ask, if the 1% difference is larger than it intuitively appears to be, is DNA good evidence of human-chimpanzee relatedness? To address that question, it is important to reflect on the fact that if humans are not related to chimpanzees, there is no reason for their DNAs to be similar at all. An infinite variety of DNA compositions are possible which could have occurred. Why should they be so similar for humans and chimpanzees?

Of course, there is always the possibility that the DNAs are so similar because of chance alone. The possible influence of chance on this event can be measured by mathematical calculations, so called *probability testing*, which has been discussed earlier. What is the mathematical probability that the 99% similarity between human and chimpanzee DNA was due to chance? This has been calculated by a statistician, Dr. Robert Abbott. The result of the calculation shows that the probability of human and chimpanzee DNA having a 99% relatedness due to chance alone is less than one in a billion! Finally, the chemical evidence of DNA relatedness is also supported by the strong archaeological evidence which shows that humans and chimpanzees had a common ancestor some 5 million years ago.

On a very practical level we need the best information available to guide and govern our lives. It would be preposterous to go against odds of one in a billion for forming our belief on a question like this which is of such vital importance to understanding ourselves and our behavior. We would certainly not bet on a race horse, have a surgical operation, or fly across an ocean if the odds of the success of the venture were less than one in a billion.

Do Humans and Higher Primates Have Self-Consciousness While Other Animals Do Not

A common experience of many persons has been to see a song bird fighting with its reflection in a window. The bird perceives the reflection as that of another bird, a presumed rival who has invaded its territory. Most species of animals on seeing their reflections have the same inability to recognize themselves. This is obvious from their behavior toward the perceived "stranger." They attempt to smell, touch, attack, or play with the image and, when possible, will go behind the reflecting surface to look for the "other animal" they have seen. Young humans under the age of approximately two years old have the same inability to recognize their reflections and show the same types of responses.

However, on growing older, humans and the higher

primates, when given the opportunity, learn that the reflection is themselves and not another individual. Human self-recognition can be accepted with good certainty and needs no proof beyond our own experience of looking into the mirror every morning. For the higher primates, the proof comes from at least three observations in the mirror experiments. First, after self-recognition occurs, the animal no longer attempts an interaction with the reflection by such actions as trying to play with or attack the image. Secondly, the animal begins to look at the image with obvious interest as it touches and examines parts of it's own body, being guided by the reflection. Finally, and most convincingly, if bright paint is placed on some part of the animal's face, this "abnormality" is recognized in the reflection. The animal immediately touches the affected area and attempts to remove the offending substance, using its reflection to guide the activity.

Other animal species do not show this type of behavior when exposed to a mirror. Thus, through observing their behavior in this situation, it is possible to conclude that the non-primate species lack the intellectual capacity for self-recognition. Other explanations for their lack of behavior indicating self-recognition – poor eye sight, lack of interest, "embarrassment" – do not make sense.

Humans also have more sophisticated forms of self-awareness that appear to be lacking in the higher primates. Humans have awareness of individual mortality. When this first appeared is not clear, but that it exists needs no special proof. As discussed earlier, archaeological evidence of ritual burials date from as far back as 50,000 years ago, suggesting perhaps the awakening of religious feelings in early humans during that period. Perhaps this event was associated with developing human awareness of self-mortality. On the other hand, extensive observational studies of the higher primates in their natural surroundings have never shown that they bury their dead or exhibit any behavior, other than sometimes showing hyperactivity during thunderstorms, that suggests any form of emerging "religious" practice. By these behavioral criteria, which appear reasonable for interpreting ideas of the human intellect, one can conclude that the non-human primates are not aware of their own mortality. Is it proper to apply the human behavioral criteria to chimpanzees? Why not? Remember, our gene composition is very closely related to the chimpanzee. Therefore, chimpanzee behavioral responses to the knowledge of self-mortality, if indeed such existed, could reasonably be expected to be similar to ours, as are other forms of their social behavior such as hunting in groups and dominance-seeking among peers.

Finally, from our knowledge of astronomy, we are aware that at some incomprehensibly distant time in the future, our sun will exhaust its nuclear fuel and die. At that time, our species, if still in existence, will also die. This knowledge of the ultimate mortality of our planet and of our species is also uniquely human. There is no evidence that higher primates have ever built a primitive astronomical observatory like Stonehenge. To believe that non-human primates have knowledge of astronomy is ridiculous. While it is obviously not much cause for personal concern for most people, knowledge of the eventual and inalterable "end of the world" does add to our human awareness of the vulnerability and transient nature of life. This kind of understanding is a recognized cause for the introspective thinking which leads to religion and philosophy which we have and the higher primates lack.

Thus, a considerable body of evidence, well founded in both everyday experience and scientific observation, has established quite conclusively that humans and higher primates have a form of self-awareness which is lacking in other animals. Furthermore, there is good reason to believe, based on extensive observational studies of the higher primates, that human self-awareness has at least two dimensions, knowledge of eventual individual mortality and knowledge of the ultimate end of our planet and species, which are not shared by the other higher primates.

Is There Evidence That Animals Lack the Intellectual Capacity for Reference?

The intellectual capacity for reference — understanding "more" and "less" – has been postulated as being essential to the development of human *standards, ideals,* and the capacity for *judgement.* To judge a distance as long, it is necessary to understand the opposite concept of short. It is obvious that humans do possess reference. This is proven by our continuous use of adjectives, adverbs, and prepositions. These are words whose purpose is to convey reference, words which modify objects, actions, or locations – *tall* man, run *fast, in* the house. In contrasting this capacity of animal and human intellect, it is necessary to seek evidence to support the belief that conscious understanding of reference is lacking in animal thought.

Animals do behave in ways which appear to show they are making choices such as to graze or hunt in one area and not in another. But this type of behavior is not necessarily a reflection of self-conscious choice and does not necessarily require a conscious understanding of reference. In the above example, the grazing or hunting opportunity only has to be present, that is "appealing," to attract the animal's attention. The hungry cow is interested in grass, and the more grass, the better. The cow cannot graze where there is no grass; also, given the opportunity, the cow will not graze where there is only a little grass. However, this behavior does not prove that the cow is using an understanding of reference – making conscious judgements – in its thinking. To explain this brings up a concept which is difficult for our human intellect to grasp because it is so foreign to the way we automatically think. This concept is that without having reference, animal thinking is by necessity totally *concrete*; thus, essentially totally positive. Thus, in the example given, "grass" is the only concept of which the cow is intellectually capable. Therefore, the only idea that can occur when the cow sees "better" grass is that the thought of grass becomes stronger "GRASS !" In other words, the idea of "grass" has been given more emotional content. We humans do the same thing, adding emotion to words to give them more emphasis instead of qualifying them by adjectives or adverbs. "Boy, am I "HUNGRY!" instead of "I am very hungry." "What a MESS!" Not "what a big mess." This emotional amplification of ideas as a forerunner to their intellectual qualification by reference is interesting in light of the report that chimpanzees are not able to vocalize in the absence of an appropriate emotional state. Without the capacity for reference, the cow's intellect is not capable of consciously conceiving of the concept of "nothing" or of associated concepts like "less." Therefore, the qualifying ideas of "less grass" or "poor grass" is beyond the cow's comprehension. All of this does not stop the cow from grazing in the area of the pasture where there is GRASS!

The intellect of some higher primates is not entirely incapable of understanding reference, only it is very poorly equipped to do so. Experiments with adult chimpanzees have shown limited ability to answer "more" and "less" questions. In an example of one experiment, it took seven months of laborious training to prepare the animal for testing. The training involved over 3000 sessions with the concept of "more" and an equal number with the concept of "less" before it was felt that the animal was prepared for the experiment. Even with the training, the level of performance was not very good. Clearly, among even the most intelligent animals such as chimpanzees, mental capacity for reference is extremely limited compared to humans.

The idea for a limitation in animal understanding of the *negative* has solid experimental support. Behavioral studies have shown that animals have great difficulty using information provided by the *absence* of something. For example, pigeons cannot learn to obtain food when a signal is removed but easily do so when a signal is added. Chimpanzees show similar inability to use *feature-negative information*, that is to recognize the absence of something which has been removed from their sensory environment. Humans show the same tendency to focus on the positive and fail to recognize the negative. A psychologist interested in this subject, Kurt Koffka, put it this way, "We normally see things and not the holes between them." However, humans do much better than the animals in seeing the holes. For example, humans would have much less trouble learning to recognize the feature-negative signal in the pigeon and chimpanzee experiments described above. Nevertheless, recognizing the negative has been a challenge for us. The invention of the mathematical concept of zero was not easy for our intellect. Notched bones, which were presumably used by our ancestors for counting, date from 20,000 to 30,000 years ago. Hieroglyphic symbols representing positive numbers were used 5000 years ago. However, it was only in the last 1500 years that the human intellect conceived of the highly sophisticated concept of zero as a term having the meaning of "nothing."

Our human understanding of "nothing" is part of the intellectual foundation on which we have built our rich repertoire of reference. Reference requires understanding graduations from the presence of something to its total absence. An intellect without the capacity to understand the concept of absence cannot think in terms of reference. Without the capacity for processing feature-negative information, ideas of references are beyond the intellect of animals.

This conjecture, while very interesting, provides no evidence for animal lack of reference in a behavioral setting. What is needed for that are observations of animal behavior which support the concept. Such an example comes from the observation of the behavior of dogs which are bred and trained as retrievers. An intelligent retriever has no difficulty in simultaneously remembering two or even three objects that it has seen fall in the field. The objects may be located at a considerable distance from the dog and may fall in high grass or other cover which hide them from the dog's view. As long as the objects are separated from each other along routes like the spokes of a wheel, the talented dog can often remember the exact location of each very well, as well or better than humans. To perform this task, the dog sits and watches each object fall in sequence. It then is sent to retrieve each in turn, returning to the starting place with each object before going to retrieve the next. Thus, the dog must remember the location of the second object, while retrieving the first, and remember the location of the third object while retrieving the first and second. However, if the objects are not widely spaced apart as described above but are all placed along only one line or nearly along one line — "over and under" — the dog has difficulty in remembering their locations. This is especially true if the dog is sent for the objects which are farthest away before it is sent for the closest object. In this situation, the dog tends to forget the closest object and run past it and hunt at a longer distance. Humans remember objects placed in this configuration much better than dogs. The dog, by its behavior, shows that it is having difficulty grasping the concept of "long" and "short." The problem is not in the dog's remembering three objects, which it has shown that it can do very well when they are placed in a widely spaced configuration. The problem is that having once gone along a certain route and having found an object at a specific location along that route, the dog cannot conceive that another object is along the same route but at a *greater or lesser* distance. The dog, by its behavior, shows that its intellect lacks the capacity for reference.

Is There Evidence That Human Intellect Has Qualitative Capacities Not Shared by Animals?

The *quantitative* differences between human and animal intellect are enormous and obvious. It is true that the standard being used for making the judgement of "enormous" is our human standard and subject to our bias and vanity. However, for those who would criticize the use of this standard, it can only be pointed out with all respect, that there is no other standard to use. Can they supply an alternative standard? A chimpanzee standard? A cow standard? The answer to this question is, obviously, "no."

And in this reply is the answer to the question posed: "Do we humans have *qualitative* differences in intellect from the animals?" *Standards, ideals, self-judgement*, what other species than humans have the intellectual capacity for such concepts? There are none. There is no creditable evidence that even the most likely candidates, the highly intelligent higher primates, have ever shown behavior suggesting this intellectual achievement. Chimpanzees, bonobos, gorillas, and orangutans have been closely observed by talented and dedicated scientists for thousands of hours in recent years. There is no report of any behavior reflecting ideation which suggests a conscious awareness of standards, ideals, and self-judgements. They do not have this intellectual capacity. Nor is there evidence for higher primates understanding causality and practicing science. We are still learning about causality ourselves. The great majority of intelligent and educated humans, if asked today, could not give an intelligent explanation of the elements of "causal inference," which is the basis of understanding scientific causation.

We have learned in recent years that animals like we — or, if you will, we like animals — communicate, make and use tools, and share some of the same emotions and, in many other ways, are similar. We also know that we and the higher primates share certain forms of self-recognition. But at the highest level of intellectual function, in our understanding and use of standards, ideals, and self-judgement, and in our understanding of causality and in the practice of science, we stand alone, we are unique. We also appear to be unique in the practice of Ethic, but the discussion of that question requires the consideration of other issues which will now be addressed.

Is There Evidence That Humans Have Free-Will Which Allows Them to Practice Ethic?

No site on the human genome has been identified which controls the understanding and practice of Ethic. Currently, the entire human genome is being mapped in a collaborative scientific project. As the Human Genome Project proceeds to completion in the next few years, it is unlikely that such a site will be identified, although it is not out of the question. Sites controlling certain types of aggressive behavior may already have been identified. If Ethic can be reduced to a chemical structure and if it can be controlled by genetic engineering, that would have to be a most remarkable human achievement. Its consequences would be unimaginable and problematic. It would bring incalculable benefits in the reduction of human misery. On the other hand, a world in which all of our lives were subject to chemical manipulation and the "free-will" of the individual would be lost is a demoralizing thought.

Since the discovery of DNA, the dialogue about the existence of human "free-will" has changed. Has it been terminated for good? The dialogue changed because chemical reactions follow predetermined and specific pathways which are not subject to the influence of an intangible force such as Ethic. Are you really in control of your actions or are they the result of chemical reactions programmed by your DNA? The knowledge of DNA raises difficult questions about the idea of free-will and the human conscience.

But we must also remember that the way in which these chemical reactions will be expressed as behavior, except with the newborn infant, is controlled in part by the prior *experience* of the individual. Experience is not programmed by the DNA because it is the result of external forces. And the experience of everyone of us is different. In life, experience does influence behavior – "once bitten, twice shy."

Also, through scientific investigation, humans are producing increasing amounts of new knowledge which greatly influences human behavior. For example, we take polio vaccine not because this behavior is programmed by our DNA and, therefore, a natural thing to do but because our intellects allowed us to perform the science which showed it is beneficial to our health. Suppose the experiments had shown that the vaccine was not beneficial; in that case, we would not be taking the vaccine. Thus, it can be seen that our thought and behavior are controlled by an interaction between the chemistry of our brain and the events we have experienced as a result of external forces. While it is true that at the molecular level chemical reactions control emotion, thought, and behavior, it is also true that prior experience with and knowledge acquired of external forces in part control the direction which these reactions take. External force is a separate factor which affects our biological system but which is not of that system.

For the present purpose, it is important to determine if there is *behavioral evidence* that free-will and conscience actually exist and that humans are capable of the practice of Ethic? Experiments based on contrived opportunities to find and return "lost" valuables have shown interesting findings. In these kind of experiments, 30% to 50% of persons will make an attempt to return a valuable such as a "lost" wallet but 20% will not. Some will ignore it. These "lost" wallet experiments are most interesting and important because they serve as an objective measure of the predictability of ethical behavior – honesty. The fact that ethical behavior, as defined by this criterion, is not uniform is in direct contradiction to the uniformity of behavior which would be expected if it were entirely controlled by a chemical reaction. Why did not all the people observed who did not ignore the lost wallet, either return it (ethical behavior) or keep it (unethical behavior) as a chemical reaction theory would predict?

I have personally observed a situation in which members of an audience were asked about their knowledge of an imaginary but supposedly important scientific study. The question was asked in such a way as to embarrass those who had to admit, by not raising their hand, that they did not know about the "important" study. Approximately 30% of the audience raised their hands, claiming to have heard of the imaginary study, thus, in effect, telling a lie. Why was there not uniform lying or uniform truth-telling, if the behavior was simply the result of a reaction programmed by the DNA?

The explanations for these interesting observations remain obscure at the present time but there are at least three hypotheses which could explain the observations. One theory, which has been raised earlier, is that only a certain proportion of our species have evolved to the point where they have the intellectual capacity to have a conscience and where their behavior conforms to Ethic. The horrible behavior of apparently sane and normal people which has been witnessed throughout history up to the present time, gives this view considerable appeal. According to this hypothesis, the DNA of some people is programmed for honest, truthful and caring behavior, having a conscience, and ethical behavior while the DNA of others lacks critical components for this, resulting in dishonesty, lying, and uncaring behavior. Thus, each group follows the chemical directive of their DNA.

A second possible explanation is that the DNA of all people

is programmed for developing sufficient self-judgmental capacity to have a "conscience" but it is not "activated" in all people or some people choose to ignore it. Depending on the state of activation of the conscience and the "virtue" or lack of virtue of the individual at the time in question, there will be honest, truthful, and caring behavior or dishonest, untruthful, and uncaring behavior. In this explanation, the concept of "virtue" implies the presence of free-will and introduces the concept of "good" and "evil." With this hypothesis, inconsistency of ethical behavior is explained as the result of differences in experience or education in awakening the conscience, or the "good" or "evil" character of the person, if the conscience is awake.

A third explanation for the inconsistent behavior described in the above examples is that conscience has a supernatural origin, making it separate and distinct from our biologic being. This explanation, by its nature, is not subject to scientific investigation and must be accepted or rejected on the basis of faith.

A final point for consideration is whether there is evidence that animals will behave in such a way as to suggest that they are capable of consciously practicing Ethic. An interesting experiment, if it could be performed, would be to do a study with chimpanzees which is similar to the "lost valuable" study described above. The design of the study would be changed so that the chimpanzee being studied would observe another member of its band appear to unknowingly drop a desirable piece of food. In this way, the chimpanzee being observed would know who was the owner of the food. What percentage of chimpanzees do you think would attempt to return the food to its owner? Based on our knowledge of animal behavior, it is reasonable to believe that none of the chimpanzees would voluntarily return the food to its owner. If this supposition is indeed true, then there is behavioral evidence that at least some humans, such as those returning the lost wallet or those telling the truth about the knowledge of the study, are qualitatively different from animals in showing evidence for the practice of Ethic. Also, the finding of variable behavior among ourselves in an ethically challenging situation is evidence that for reasons, yet unclear, we are not all alike in this regard.

PRACTICE OF HUMAN BEHAVIOR

Understanding What Makes
a Person Human

Humans consciously attempt to adhere to a standard of behavior; animals do not.

Introduction

Pervasiveness of Our Animal Behavior

Each one of us – ever since we could understand the meaning of the word "human" – have known that as individuals, *human is what we are*. And since we are humans, everything we do must be a human activity. Right? Actually, that is not really correct. Let's look at what do we do in a typical day. We get up, perform our bodily functions, groom, and eat a meal. But animals do the same thing. Animals do that just as routinely as we humans do. Then we go to work to make a living. Animals do that also. Hunting and gathering food is an animal's form of work. After work, we like to relax, socialize, and play. Animals do all of these things. When given the opportunity, animals in captivity can even learn to drink a beer and like it. So, have we spent all of our hypothetical day in strictly animal activities? In a way, yes. And yet, despite all of the similarities in basic behavior we share with animals, a person living in downtown Tokyo has a style of living which is obviously very different from an orangutan living in the jungles of Borneo. It is the lifestyle which is the most obvious difference between us and animals, but is it the lifestyle which actually sets us apart?

Human Behavior Does Not Arise from Having Advanced Technology

What makes our lifestyle and that of animals so different? The major reason for the glaringly obvious differences between the lifestyles is *technology*. That is, our tools, machines, and buildings and the use we make of them are so much more advanced than with animals. For example, chimpanzees are limited to the use of very primitive tools like a straw to poke in a hole when fishing for termites, and chimpanzees can only build crude nests in trees. We humans have an almost infinite variety of sophisticated tools, machines, buildings, and weapons. To expand on the list of these things would be boring, but to put the issue in perspective, let's consider a motorcycle. Now a motorcycle is not a very sophisticated human tool, but it is totally beyond the intellectual capacity of a chimpanzee to invent one. But isn't it interesting that chimpanzees in animal shows have been taught to ride small motorcycles? A much more sophisticated human tool is the computer. Inventing a computer is wildly beyond the intellectual capacity of a monkey, but isn't it also interesting that a monkey can be taught to play games on a computer? Does the animal that learns to ride a motorcycle or play a computer game suddenly become a human? Of course not. Does a human who rides a motorcycle or uses a computer prove by doing these things that he or she has the unique intellectual qualities of a human? No. In truth, the human has done nothing the animal couldn't and didn't do. Thus, the *use* of sophisticated tools and machines, while of practical value and impressive, is really not very good evidence for a claim to being human. This is not to say that human intellect was not involved in the *invention* of these wonderful things. But inventing and using are two different things.

Relationship to the Use of Tools Similar in Animals and Humans

We do experience great emotional satisfaction and pride in having and using these remarkable things – the super sky scrapers, the mega bridges, the endless highways – and in our marvelous machines – the jumbo jet planes, the space rockets, the computer controlled assembly lines – and it feeds our vanity. Yet, without our practicing Ethic, having and using these very wonderful things, only makes us super animals, not humans. Now animals cannot possibly have invented these things. But that is not the point. The point is that these things, despite their complexity and sophistication, are still – when we use them – in the category of tools. They have the same relationship to us as the straw for fishing for termites does to the chimpanzee. They do not help us think and behave like human beings. They do not help us practice Ethic any more than the straw helps the chimpanzee practice Ethic. Their *use* does not provide the standard for distinguishing between animal and human behavior. That's the point. What advanced technology does is give us enormous previously undreamed of physical power and material riches, but it does not direct or control how that power or those riches will be used, constructively through Ethic or in a destructive way associated with the animal side of our nature.

Civilized Behavior Is Not Necessarily Human Behavior

By the same standard, being "civilized" and "cultured" does not necessarily equate with being human. If being civilized means having a good education, gourmet dining, wearing stylish clothes, and having an appreciation of "culture" but does not include understanding and practicing Ethic, it also is no more than a sophisticated form of animal behavior. To get through life pleasantly and prosperously, believing we are "civilized" feeds our vanity and mistakenly makes us believe we are behaving like sophisticated *humans*. However, sophistication in material matters has nothing to do with practicing Ethic and being human. That is not to say that some sophisticated people do not practice Ethic and are human, because they are. But their being human has nothing to do with the fact that they are sophisticated.

If you happen to be in a fine restaurant with its elegant furnishings and stylish ritual, look around you at the people and think about what they are doing. They are having a wonderful time eating, drinking, displaying, gossiping, and possibly getting ready to go to the theater or a concert to be entertained. In short, being healthy and happy animals having a good time. There is nothing undesirable or "wrong" about this type of behavior. That is what the animal side of our nature was born and bred to do. Nothing that is, unless we fool ourselves into thinking that this type of behavior alone makes us superior humans and, therefore, that it is a worthy ethical goal.

Human Behavior in Everyday Life

So what are the activities of everyday life which make humans different from animals? This is in some ways the wrong question. The difference lies more in how and why we do things in relation to other people than in what we do. How we treat other people and how we use the full power of our intellect to understand why things happen. The difference lies in using Ethic to guide our behavior and using human understanding of causation in decision making and scientific practice.

How do these things actually fit into our real life behavior? First, it is important to realize and accept that because of our biological nature, we have to spend a large amount of our time attending to our animal needs. Also, to make our lives enjoyable, we spend a considerable amount of time fulfilling our animal desires. The subject of asceticism, avoiding "the desires of the flesh" to focus on spiritual matters, and of its philosophical limitations will be discussed in more detail later. For the present, we should recognize that while some of us may choose to lead a life devoted to philosophic and religious contemplation – with avoidance of material things as much as possible – most of us will continue to live fully in the material world. "You are right about that" you say, "and that kind of lifestyle takes up most of my time – the family, work, TV, shopping. I don't have time for those other things you are talking about." But that view is incorrect. Adding Ethic and human understanding of causation to your lifestyle *does not require that you spend extra time and effort in your everyday activities* – you may spend less. After all, telling the truth is usually easier and less time consuming than lying, and really understanding why things happen makes life easier. What it means is that you conduct your everyday activities in possibly a different way than you have been by practicing Ethic and using human understanding of causation when possible in interpreting events and making decisions. Then you are practicing human behavior.

Practical Advantages of Human Behavior

As discussed above, *using* sophisticated tools does not meet the standard of unique human behavior, inventing new tools through scientific experimentation does. Most of us are not practicing scientists, but that does not mean that understanding causation is not important to our personal lives. This is not a put down of non-scientists. It is an encouragement for all of us to use our full intellectual power to think "smarter," for our own good and the good of others. Not letting yourself be fooled, if you can help it. In everyday life we are faced with evaluating "facts" and making decisions. Do we or do we not drink coffee because of health concerns? Is what this political candidate says about the crime rate true? Does this new product really do what the advertisement claims? For dealing with this side of life, understanding causation is invaluable.

Once the concepts of causality are understood, it does not consume more of an individual's time but like Ethic, leads to a different approach to everyday life. What is important is to use this knowledge when you can, and also to know when you *lack* sufficient information to reach a sound conclusion. Being aware that you lack essential information for reaching an understanding does two important things. It tends to reduce the level of emotion involved in thinking about the issue and, thus, reduces the risk of destructive behavior. It also motivates you to seek the information which is lacking. Both of these are very important human attitudes.

Limits of Causal Analysis

It is important to remember that certain ideas are not subject to causal analysis. Philosophical and religious beliefs based on faith are not testable by this standard. Knowing and understanding this principle is important for developing another important human attitude, *tolerance*, of other people and of their spiritual and philosophic beliefs. Most humans agree on the same material and spiritual goals – kindness, happiness, peace, lack of want. Selecting the methods for attaining these goals is what causes most of the problems. The goals are not subject to causal analysis. The means of achieving the goals are.

Summary

We rarely give serious consideration to what makes us human in our everyday lives because we automatically assume that everything we are doing is human in character. But as discussed in this book, critical analysis reveals that most "human" activities are shared with animals. Only a relatively small proportion of our thinking and activities qualitatively set us apart from the animals. For someone to merit respect as a human requires their showing two things. One is the understanding and practice of Ethic. This implies not just the self-conscious awareness of their own behavior, but the judgement based on that awareness that practicing Ethic is desirable. Many people have the intellectual capacity for the first part, but for reasons that are not yet clear, do not show evidence of the second.

The second requirement of being human is an understanding of causality and its use in the practice of Ethic. The attempted practice of Ethic which is not based on accurate and logical interpretation of events is flawed and may be harmful. Likewise, understanding and acting on causality but not practicing Ethic is not a form of human behavior. The standard of being human requires both.

It is generally well understood that intelligent and successful people may not be ethical in their behavior – smart, successful villains are a stock item in literature and entertainment. But it is not as well appreciated that people who sincerely care about others may fail in their ethical responsibilities by deliberately neglecting or ignoring their intellectual capacity for logical thinking and an understanding of causation. Good intentions in caring about others do not make up for the harm that may result from illogical and superstitious behavior. Deliberately neglecting to take advantage of our full intellectual capacity because of peer pressure or other reasons is an animal way of behaving.

The Personal Importance
of This Knowledge

I can make a living telling the truth

Casey Stengel, contemporary

The Personal Importance of This Knowledge

Understanding the dual nature of human thought and behavior has obvious implications for your own behavior. Because all humans have self-awareness, we assume that all are capable of self-judgement and have developed an inherent sense of what is "right" and "wrong," a conscience. If you have this kind of self-awareness, you have the means – if not the will – for behaving in a human way. The quotation which introduces this chapter is from Casey Stengel who was a baseball manager. He said..."I can make a living telling the truth." What he meant by that was he lived his life in a truthful way. He did not lie to his associates, although at times telling the truth might have been a disadvantage to him. He was able to behave like a human and still be successful in material matters.

Options for Your Own Behavior

Unlike an animal, if you have a conscience you have options for how to think about and treat others. You can behave like an animal yourself and treat others like animals ("it's a jungle out there," "what goes around comes around"). You can behave like an animal and treat others like naive humans ("fleece the suckers." "If you're not cheating, you're not trying"). You can behave like a human and on occasion and through necessity treat others like animals (sometimes required for self-preservation). And you can behave like a human whenever possible and treat others like humans with honesty, fairness, respect, and caring, the true goal of Ethic.

Life Goals

The major goal in life for many people is to become a clever, successful animal, although they do not see it as such. They seek to obtain glamorous, well paid jobs, positions of power, and to travel and be seen in the "right places" with the "right people." "To have it made." To rise above "the common herd."

Now this is a perfectly normal and acceptable goal for the animal side of our nature. However, persons who achieve these goals often mislead themselves and others into thinking that through these kinds of successes they have become superior *humans*. Not so. They may, in fact, be superior to the common herd – of animals – but achieving "superior" human status rests on other accomplishments which are discussed in this book and which center on the practice of Ethic as based on human understanding of causality.

For true humans, the fact of being human is satisfaction enough in their lives. True humans do not feel the need to try to be superior to anybody regardless of the worth of their own material accomplishments or the recognition they receive from the world.

Being Honest with Yourself

You need to admit to yourself that your own thinking and behavior are never entirely "human" or even often "human." You are constantly and naturally displaying the animal side of your nature. The old expression, "it's only *human* nature" to excuse an unwanted behavior is incorrect. Actually, it should be "it's only the *animal* side of our nature." You can't escape the continuing animal side of your nature and, historically, if you are like most of us, *you have been unable or unwilling to recognize it for what it is*. Our use of the expression "it is only *human* nature" shows that to be true. But, most importantly, in spite of the animal side of our nature, if we have a *conscience*, we have a choice of how we behave. The personal importance of the message in this book is to lead you to examine your own intellect, to honestly determine if you are capable of self-judgement. Do you have a conscience? And, if you do, do you use it to guide you in the practice of Ethic?

Implications for Our Species

All is vanity

Ecclesiastes, 2300 years ago
(4,997,700 HO)

Implications for Our Species

Creation Myths Have an Overpowering Influence on Our Thinking

Our intellects have been and are the continuing victims of the creation myths of our tribal origins. The myths are about when we "humans" first appeared in the world – distinct, complete, and pure in our being – at least in theory if not always in our practice. But we see imperfection as the fault of personal weakness not of our prototypical design. The creation myths fuel our *vanity* and shape our unconscious beliefs about ourselves. In creation myths, the prototypical design – from the very first model – is of human purity. For example, in the Judeo-Christian version, "God created man *in his own image*." The Creation Myth – it is such a powerful force in human thinking that it should be called *The Myth*. The Myth has held and continues to hold our intellect in a form of bondage which prevents it from escaping outside of itself sufficiently to behold and *believe* in the continuing animal side of our being. Perhaps it is accurate to say that The Myth is really an integral – hardwired – part of our emotion which is so strong that the weaker force of our intellect cannot dislodge it. We resist Darwinian science as it applies to us. Sure our brain tells us we are part animal – But! But in our guts, in our heart of hearts, in our soul of souls, in our deepest inner self, in our everyday look in the mirror, "hello pal, self," we don't believe a word of it. What! Me? Impossible! Me, human! *And yet, accepting the continuing animal side of our being is the one and only explanation that makes any sense for explaining the full range of destructive "human" behavior – world history, my behavior, your behavior. It alone provides us with an understanding of ourselves and of the events of the world in all their gory detail. It alone provides a basis for our engaging in less destructive behavior in the future.* We need this understanding of ourselves for ourselves.

The Threat of This New Knowledge to How We See Ourselves

Does having the sure knowledge of the continuing animal side of our nature lower us as a species or make us less than we traditionally have believed we are? The simple answer is no, because in reality, we have never been anything but what we are. But the answer is more complicated since perception may influence behavior and, thus, influence reality. Our highest human goals and aspirations are historically based on beliefs of human uniqueness and distinction from the animals. To totally lose this belief would be damaging to our self-respect and dignity.

The New Knowledge Is Helpful to Us

Our historic belief of total distinction from the animals – human purity – is a fiction of our vanity as expressed in The Myth of our creation. But, on the other hand, the truth of our uniqueness as humans is also an indisputable fact. No animal, not even the higher primates, practices Ethic or science. And there is no good reason to think that they ever will in the finite life span of the earth. Evolution does not appear to work that way.

Our highest spiritual aspirations and our grandest scientific dreams need not be diminished by our awareness of the continuing animal side of our nature. It is sadly obvious that the destructive elements in our animal nature frequently stand in the way of our human accomplishments and we would do better if we could control them. On the positive side, our animal activities are a large part of our remarkable material accomplishments and as such, they supply us with most of the zest and enjoyment of everyday life. Without them our lives would be very dull and insipid, indeed. We must not be ashamed of our animal origins. This knowledge does not threaten our aspirations and ideals; indeed, this understanding helps us reach our higher human goals.

Conditions Affecting
Human Behavior

By a lie a man throws away and, as it
were, annihilates his dignity as a man

Immanuel Kant, 250 years ago
(4,999,750 HO)

Conditions Affecting Human Behavior

External Events Affect Ethical Behavior

What are the conditions which affect the human side of our intellect? Which are uplifting and nurture our human dignity and which are degrading and annihilate it? Experience shows that concern with truthfulness, honesty, and caring is not related to a particular individual's sex, race, or national origin. However, there are outside factors which appear to influence human thought and behavior. Conditions such as tranquility, solitude, contemplation, prayer, and suffering have traditionally been shown to stimulate thinking at a high intellectual and ethical level. On the other hand, extreme biological need and conditions which elicit strong emotion may suppress our human intellect and behavior. As discussed earlier, emotion often elicits animal behavior at the expense of human attitudes. The conditions leading to such emotions include danger, hunger, privation, sexual attraction, the need to dominate, and peer pressure. Because of our continuing animal nature, we are strongly influenced by the actions of others and our conscience is weakened so that we "join the crowd" or "don't give a damn and do it." It is especially hard for children and teenagers who have only recently emerged from the pure animal state of their early childhood to resist this pressure. Perhaps most important of all is opportunity. The ease with which we succumb to opportunity shows how delicate our ethical balance is in our current state of development.

Ethical Behavior Varies Among Individuals

Not all individuals subjected to these conditions of stress or opportunity will succumb to their effects. Real life displays of human heroism in dangerous situations and honesty in conditions of opportunity are well documented and not uncommon. Also, evidence from the "lost" valuable experiments described earlier indicate that a proportion of people are honest, as defined by this criterion, while another proportion are dishonest. Does this mean that only some people are human at the present time, and if so, should we try to distinguish them from the others? These kinds of questions are discussed next.

Practical Questions Regarding Our Animal Behavior

The human charioteer drives his (winged horses) in a pair; and one of them is noble and of noble breed, and the other is ignoble and of ignoble breed; and the driving of them of necessity gives a great deal of trouble to him

Plato, 2400 years ago
(4,997,600 HO)

Practical Questions Regarding Our Animal Behavior

Historical Recognition of Our Dual Nature

Great intellects of both the West and the East have appreciated the dual nature of the forces controlling human behavior and of the "trouble" this causes. Plato compared the problem of controlling the human *psyche* to that of driving a chariot driven by two winged horses, one manageable, the other unmanageable, and pointed out that the "vicious steed" which "has not been thoroughly trained" often caused a wreck. Tung Chung-shu, a Chinese philosopher, wrote that just as there was the belief that natural powers are controlled by the yin – the negative and destructive force – and the yang – the positive and constructive force – so to "the person also has his dual nature of humanity and greed."

Destructive Behavior Raises Practical Questions

Recognizing our dual nature raises difficult and disturbing practical questions that have not been addressed in the context of the ideas expressed in this book. What should we think of people who turn their back on the opportunity to show the human side of their nature? What about the people who did not return the "lost" money in the experiments described in the preceding section? In view of the continuing historical record of atrocious human behavior, it is not unreasonable to ask if all people actually possess a human side to their nature. Has the uniquely human part of the intellect evolved in everyone, or are there some people who lack these characteristics and are, thus, incapable of thinking and behaving like humans? Is capacity for self-judgement in the genes of each of us? Currently, there is no scientific basis for measuring this or for quantifying the capacity for practicing Ethic. Should we try to develop tests for this? And how much of understanding Ethic is not hereditary but is learned and passed on from one generation to the next? Is a display of destructive animal behavior ever excusable even if not tolerable? Just as we cannot condemn a hungry lion, who is intellectually incapable of understanding Ethic, for the "unethical" behavior of assaulting a zebra, can we hold accountable a person who lacks the intellectual capacity required for the development of a conscience? Although it is obvious, we must protect ourselves and society against this kind of individual. And supposing that once someone is judged to be possessed of only an animal nature, should they be held to a lower standard and treated differently?

The Emotional and Political Consequences of These Questions

These kinds of questions obviously have the potential to produce alarm and anger in persons who are unable or unwilling to address the existence and continuing influence of our animal nature. Also, our laws have traditionally been applied to all persons equally. Although it is interesting that different standards are sometimes applied to the same crime, for example, the crime of killing someone. The more serious "human" crime of premeditated murder receives a more severe punishment than the less severe "animal" crime of manslaughter associated with sudden uncontrollable rage.

From a practical point of view, the idea of testing ourselves to separate the "human" humans from the "animal" humans is politically out of the question even if it were possible. For one thing, the "animal" humans could be in the majority and may, therefore, control the vote. The Prince of Han was a philosopher whose writings contributed to a Legalist view in Chinese philosophy. He probably would have agreed with this assessment. He pointed out that although "people loved his (Confucius') doctrine of humanity, only 70 people became his devoted pupils. The reason is that *few people value humanity* and it is difficult to practice righteousness" (emphasis added). In Han's view, most people did not care whether they were animals or not. Now this is a most disturbing and important question to which we do not have an answer. *Do most people not really care whether they are animals or humans, or do they want to be humans and through weakness and the use of denial and hypocrisy maintain the belief that they are human, while thinking and acting like animals? If you care, it is important for you to know when your thoughts and activities are being controlled by your animal side and when they are controlled by your human side. If you stop and think about this, would you know?*

Evaluating Behavior

I feel that human beings should treat
human beings like human beings

Richard Feynman, contemporary

Evaluating Behavior

While it may not be practical or desirable to devise tests to determine who does or does not meet the standard of being a "human" human, it is worthwhile to be familiar with the qualities that an individual needs to meet this standard. For a beginning, you must have the understanding that it is desirable to tell the truth, to be honest and to treat others as you, yourself, wish to be treated. This does not mean that you never in your life tell a lie or steal, or are uncaring or cruel to others. What it does mean is that if you have a conscience and know these activities are wrong, having done them, you regret having done them and try to avoid such behavior in the future.

Evidence of Animal Behavior

To believe that because these undesirable actions are so common, which they are, and because "everybody does them," which they do, makes it all right for you to do them does not put you in the human group. If deceiving people *does not bother you*, you are a pure animal. If stealing from people *does not bother you*, you are a pure animal. If being uncaring and cruel to other people *does not bother you*, you are a pure animal. Doing these things makes you a pure animal not because this book says so or not because philosophical or religious teaching says so, but because that is how animals actually do behave towards each other in real life. Animals do not care because animals do not know any better. People who do not care because they lack a conscience are functioning on an animal level. People who behave like animals are found in all walks of life. Some have very high levels of intelligence — animal intelligence — but they lack the intellectual capacity that would make them human.

Response to Animal Behavior of Others

When people behave in a way that is destructive or harmful to you, it is not unreasonable to ask them if they have a conscience. If they respond in a way which leads you to believe that they do have a conscience, then ask them why they are not using it to direct their behavior. If they do not appear to have an understanding of Ethic or to possess a conscience, then you must adjust your own behavior accordingly to protect yourself and others from their animal nature and behavior. Do not let their charm, position, or other extraneous qualities deter you from a calm and reasoned evaluation of their nature. You can still like them, but you should not have unrealistic expectations about their future behavior.

Practicing Ethic Requires Courage

All of these things are not easy. All of these things are not popular. All of these things require the *courage* of our animal heritage. Ironically, without our animal courage to do the correct thing, to follow Ethic, we are not complete humans. We have no robustness, we have no strength, we have no *power*. Ethic requires *powerful commitment and powerful implementation*. Ethic arises from the intellect, but it's implementation and support requires our animal flesh and blood.

And we must clearly understand where the power, the strength, the commitment, and the courage are directed. The power, the strength, the commitment, the courage are directed at *ourselves, not at others*. Its target is our own capacity for self-judgement. Its goal is to supply the strength our conscience requires to overcome our powerful hardwired needs and emotions and the displeasure or ridicule of other people who are behaving like animals. We use an animal quality, courage, to help our human intellect prevail against our animal emotions. It takes real courage to withstand peer pressure. It takes real courage to turn away from easy, dishonest profit. It takes real courage to tell truths that hurt or embarrass ourselves. It takes real courage to defend the weak and helpless against attack. In fact, the paradoxical truth is that it *takes a very large amount of pure animal courage to behave like a true human being*.

Can Human Qualities
Be Learned?

Where could I escape from myself?

Augustine, 1600 years ago
(4,998,400 HO)

Can Human Qualities Be Learned?

Tung Chung-shu, mentioned earlier, was a confucianist philosopher of powerful intellect who lived approximately 2000 years ago. In describing human nature, he pointed out that in Chinese "The term "people" (min) is derived from the term "sleep" (ming)." In this he said, "Man's nature may be compared to the eyes. In sleep they are shut and there is darkness. They must await the awakening before they can see. Before the awakening it may be said that they possess the basic substance to see, but it cannot be said they see...Both nature (intellect) and feelings, which are sources of evil, are the same in a state of sleep."

A most important question to be asked about ourselves is can we learn to develop human qualities if we do not have them or can we awaken them if we do. Can we ever stop the interminable interracial, intersectional, and interreligious fighting and carnage which has been the spiritual cancer of our species?

Self-Recognition Alone Is Insufficient for the Development of Conscience

After approximately two years of age, normal children can recognize themselves in a mirror, so we all possess self-recognition. But so do chimpanzees and other higher primates who do not practice recognizable ethical behavior, so physical self-recognition alone is insufficient to provide a working conscience.

Awakening of Conscience with Adversity

How the conscience has developed in humans remains unknown. History tells of remarkable persons who were possessed of a strong conscience and who "awakened" the conscience of others. Also, there are numerous examples of persons having deep emotional, often religious, experiences which led to an ethical awakening. St. Patrick's spirituality developed during a six-year period when he endured great hardship as a slave. These kinds of examples suggest that a conscience may be present in an individual but that it may lie dormant until awakened. In such an individual, the conscience may be activated under certain conditions, but it is not clear that in the absence of a conscience one can be created. Discounting the problem of communication, the most eloquent and persuasive of sermons could not be expected to elicit ethical awareness in a chimpanzee or in a two-year old human for that matter. The chimpanzee and young child can be *trained* to avoid certain undesirable types of behavior, but that is a different process from creating a conscience.

Possible Roles of Wonder and Humility

Humans alone on this planet have an understanding of the universe which is yet another difference from all of the animals. Astronomy is one of the great, early human accomplishments. Our knowledge of astronomy has provided us with a cosmic self-consciousness which inspires us with a unique sense of wonder and awe that can be overpowering. *Perhaps part of the essential ingredients of a conscience are self-awareness combined with such a sense of overpowering wonder and awe.* We alone have experienced both! We alone know our awful isolation and vulnerability on a tiny speck of dust in an inconceivably immense and violent universe of space and time. Acquiring humility was the price we paid and the reward we received for this knowledge. Perhaps humility was the catalyst that lead to our ethical behavior. When one becomes humble, it is easy to tell the truth, to be honest, and to be fair and compassionate. With true humility, ethical behavior becomes a source of deep reward to the individual.

Understanding May Strengthen Conscience

As pointed out earlier, the development of human intellectual capacity for self-judgement has taken place during only the last 0.1% of our existence as a species. It is not surprising that conscience is still a weak and uncertain force in most of our lives. We can hope that understanding our own true dual natures, animal and human, will give each of us a better insight into what governs our thinking and behavior, and that through this insight our individual consciences may be strengthened. It is also hoped that as a species through our shared understanding of this knowledge and through our shared commitment to its full understanding by all, a better environment will be created for human thought and behavior to flourish.

Animal vs Human
Government

As things are, any wretch who
wants to can stand up and
obtain what is good for him.

        Anonymous Athenian, 2400 years ago
                   (4,997,600 HO)

We hold these truths to be self evident
that all men are created equal.

        Thomas Jefferson, 300 years ago
                 (4,999,700 HO)

Animal Versus Human Forms of Government

The Animal Origin of Government

The social organization of many animal species is based on *dominance*. For example, chimpanzee bands are controlled by an "alpha" male member of the group who establishes dominance over all other members of the group. This is accomplished by violence and threats of violence towards the other members of the group. The first human political systems originated in the same way, with tribal chiefs and later kings and dictators acquiring power by physical and psychological dominance over the members of their groups. Some contemporary humans have inherited and still live under this animal type of government which has been institutionalized over time by various rituals and laws.

A very early Irish poem describes this form of government. The poem is about the petty kings who successively occupied a small dirt fort in Kildare.

"The fort opposite the oak wood —
Once it was Bruidge's, it was Cathal's,
It was Aed's, it was Ailills',
It was Conaing's, it was Cuilińe's,
And it was Maeldúine's —
The fort remains after each in his turn,
And the kings asleep in the ground."

The human names in the poem can be replaced by the names given the dominant males who successively led a band of chimpanzees which was studied along Lake Tanganyika in Africa. The poem does not lose its poignant meaning.

The valleys along the great lake —
Once they were Goliath's, they were Mike's,
They were Humphrey's, they were Figan's,
And they were Goblin's —
The valleys remain after each in his turn,
And the ape kings asleep in the mold.

Emergence of a Human Form of Government

Perhaps in part because of the sentiment expressed in the poem, the recognition of the ultimate fallibility of even the most mighty, a radically different form of government appeared. In the classical Greek city states, the human intellect conceived a new and uniquely human system which has led to contemporary democracy. Greek democracy is considered to have started in Athens 2500 years ago with Cleisthenes' reforms. Not long after its invention, an unknown Athenian writer gave the new form of government the grudging approval recorded on the introductory page to this section. In recent times, the words of that great intellect, Thomas Jefferson, gave democracy a special lustre.

With Human Government, Power Resides in the Governed

With this new system, the fallibility of the solitary leader was recognized and the governing power was distributed among the individuals of the group. Political choices were no longer made by the dominant individual but by the collective will of some of the individual members of the group as expressed in a majority opinion. With time, this "voting franchise" has been extended to all members of some contemporary societies. This type of governance is a uniquely human achievement.

Continuing Conflict Between Animal and Human Government

Both the animal form of government, based on domination by a single individual, and the human form of government, based on political equality of the governed exist on earth at the present time. These systems have frequently been in active competition, often in the form of physical violence, or war, as we term this activity. Humans supporting *human* political values have established democracies through armed revolution against humans supporting animal political tradition, and humans supporting animal tradition have sometimes overthrown democratic governments supported by humans who through weakness or apathy were defeated. Voting, when done under the guidance of Ethic, is a uniquely human form of behavior; voting out of narrow self-interest puts one among the animals. Voting for leaders, who practice Ethic, when such people are available, makes good human sense.

Animal and Human Qualities of Leaders

Emotion, not intellect, unfortunately, continues to have the controlling influence over choice of leaders for many or most people. Thus, a major problem in human governance is that most aspiring leaders cannot gain power without having the animal magnetism and charisma needed to attract armed followers or gain the confidence of voters. Unfortunately, these animal characteristics do not guarantee the presence of the human qualities needed to provide good leadership once power is obtained. History suggests that leaders with both of these qualities have not been very common. It should be obvious to anyone who has read this far in the book that corruption in government — using political power for personal gain — is a type of self-defining animal behavior.

Learning, Teaching, and Training

The mind should be an instrument
and not a receptacle

                        Electors of Oriel College, 250 years ago
                                     (4,999,750 HO)

Learning, Teaching, and Training

Animals Teach and Train Other Animals

    Animals are capable of both learning and teaching. Good animal mothers teach their young important skills which are needed for their success in life. The mother cat brings crippled prey to her kittens to teach them how to hunt. Animals also learn from watching other animals who may be unrelated as kin. Animals do these things without self-awareness and, of course, do not formalize the process by going to school. Also, animals, unlike humans, do not have the ability to acquire and store knowledge purely for knowledge's sake, that is, knowledge that has no immediate apparent practical application.
    Thus, teaching per se originated as an animal activity, and much of its content is still of an animal nature. However, the content may be in the category of uniquely human ideas when the subjects are such things as Ethic, logic, and causality. This is not to say that teaching the liberal arts has not been essential for human development. Rhetoric, literature, and history have roots in our animal origins, but they have served to express and disseminate the great ideas and ideals of our intellect on which rests our humanity. Also, practical subjects and vocational skills are important for us since humans have to make a living, just like cats.
    Training is also an activity with origins in our animal nature. In a crude sense, the lion "trains" other animals to stay away from its kill by assaults and threats of assaults. It suppresses the unwanted behavior of hyenas and vultures who become "trained" to patiently sit and wait until the lion leaves the kill.

Human Use of Education

    When used in a proper human way, education and training should strengthen the intellectual "instrument" described in the quotation introducing this chapter. Thus, the goal of education and training is to produce a more powerful functional intellect. An educated human should not be just a precocious scholar crammed with sterile facts, but an intellectual force directed by a human standard of behavior – by Ethic. Also, education should not be used only as a means of improving our animal craftiness in taking advantage of others, which is too often what results from graduate education in the professional schools.

Legal System Based on Animal Heritage

It is important to recognize that a person who is being forced to do something, no matter how good the intention or how worthy the goal – wearing seat belts, going through metal detectors – is being treated like an animal and their human dignity is *being lowered*. This point deserves considerable emphasis because this legalistic approach of training through coercion diminishes our most precious commodity, our humanity.

It can be argued that if humans are not forced to do these things – vaccinate their children, conserve water – they would not do them at all or they would take "too long" to adopt their use. This is incorrect. If *animals* – not *humans* – were not forced to do these kinds of things they would not do them. Humans will do them because first, they understand the principles of causality and, thus, are able to accurately assess their value; and secondly, they will do them through their practice of Ethic – because of their benefit.

We may in our collective wisdom wish, at times, to force these things on people, but when we do, we need to admit to ourselves that this implies that we believe that many people are animals who must be trained. If not, such laws and regulations would not be necessary. If we value our individual and collective humanity, we should be very careful in what things we force on people. We have to remain continuously aware of the stiff price we pay when we elect to do this.

Thus, our system of laws and legal punishments is a sophisticated form of animal training. Animal training may employ both the negative reinforcement associated with punishment and the positive reinforcement of reward, and our laws reflect this understanding. In either event, the "trainer" — the law maker and the law enforcer — are engaging in an activity which reflects the continuing animal side of our nature. Systems of law remain necessary to control the destructive animal behavior of some people, and the rule of law under a democratic form of government is preferable to the law of the jungle, but it is not superior to the dictates of an enlightened conscience practicing Ethic.

Teaching the Principle of Ethic

We do not know how important teaching the principle of Ethic is in awakening the conscience. It may be very important. It is possible that without instruction, many people will not on their own develop an understanding of the principle. Based on this assumption, our teachers must teach what it means to be truly human and what it means to be animal. And they must point out destructive animal behavior when it occurs. Our teachers must teach what Ethic is. Our teachers must believe in Ethic. Our teachers must live Ethic to the best of their individual abilities if they are to fulfill their important responsibility as role models as well as conveyors of information.

FACTORS AFFECTING INTELLECTUAL FUNCTION

Pathologic Thought and Behavior

The sleep of reason produces monsters

Francisco Goya, 200 years ago
(4,999,800 HO)

Pathologic Thought and Behavior

Not all human thought and behavior are normal. It is important to recognize when destructive behavior is the result of mental illness. The legal definitions of sanity have historically used the standard of knowing "right" from "wrong." This standard is based on the assumption that all "normal" persons have a working conscience and in the absence of one, can be considered mentally impaired. As has been discussed earlier, this assumption — based on the myth of human purity — is at least subject to question and as a point of fact, little scientific inquiry has ever been made into the question.

Pathologic Thought Does Not Conform to Reality

Nevertheless, mental illness is a reality which has been well described by medical science although not necessarily well understood. Central to the nature of mental illness is a disturbance of thought, so that the perceptions of the affected individual do not accurately reflect the reality of events. The abnormal thinking is usually associated with ideas of self-perception. With depression, it is a feeling of loss, guilt, shame, worthlessness, and hopelessness, in which our natural animal optimism is not operative. Schizophrenia is characterized by delusional ideas involving feelings of persecution or inappropriate feelings of grandeur. Blunting of normal animal emotion, the so called "flat affect," is a common feature of this form of mental illness.

Emotional and Intellectual Components

These features of both depression and schizophrenia suggest that these diseases are in part affecting the emotion. In fact, they are commonly referred to as "emotional illness." However, the psychological dynamics and behavioral results of depression and of schizophrenia are different. With depression, the important element of guilt or shame is often based on an inappropriate self-judgement relative to some standard of behavior. The most serious end result of depression is self-destruction. Because of the self-judgmental aspect of depression, the intellect appears to play a role in the process. In some ways, depression could be considered the result of hyperactivity of the conscience. The refractory nature of the emotional component of mental illness is shown by the fact that persons with mental illness are not susceptible to change through logical persuasion. Psychotherapy and new chemical treatments are changing the prognosis of mental illness.

Causes Destructive Behavior

With schizophrenia, persecutory and aggrandizing ideation may result in destructive behavior towards others. When this disorder has occurred in persons in positions of great power, it has resulted in some of the bloodiest tyrants in human history. With such individuals, there has been no practical recourse except physical restraint or extermination. It continues to be of the highest importance to prevent individuals with these types of mental illness from obtaining positions of uncontrolled power. History has shown the indescribable horrors which can occur when certain types of insane individuals come to power.

Preventing Persons with Pathologic Intellects Obtaining Power Is Important

When Thomas Jefferson spoke of the "illimitable freedom of the human mind" he had in mind the constructive and uplifting goals of which our intellects are capable. In this century, we have witnessed the illimitable freedom of the deranged human mind to pursue destructive and horribly degrading goals. However, it is by no means certain that all such "monsters" are deranged. Instead, some of history's tyrants may, in fact, have been normal people who lacked a conscience and were only exhibiting the bloody and "sadistic" features of a pure animal nature.

Irrespective of the cause, *we must make this knowledge a permanent part of human self-awareness.* We must use the standard of Ethic to recognize this aberration whenever and wherever it appears. We can no longer allow ourselves to be misled by animalistic charisma and pandering to our own animal hungers and emotions. Tyrants rise to power by such means and by trying to conceal their destructive intentions until it is too late to effectively oppose them. We should not support leaders unless they show *convincing evidence that they have the capacity and willingness to practice Ethic.* Their past record, especially in small matters, is an important indication of their true intentions. We will have less chance of being misled if we will judge their actions and not their words.

Mind-Altering Drugs

Inflamming wine, pernicious to mankind

                      Homer, 2100 years ago
                           (4,997,990 HO)

I was drunk

Mind-Altering Drugs

We have a long history of using mind-altering drugs that goes back well into our animal beginnings. African elephants get drunk on certain fruits which ferment in their digestive system. Chimpanzees have been reported to spontaneously develop a taste for alcohol from eating fermented fruit. Members of ancient civilizations used mind-altering drugs.

Adverse Effect on Intellect and Ethic

The use of mind-altering drugs covers a wide spectrum from the innocuous glass or two of wine with meals to the destructive or self-destructive use of "hard" drugs in other categories. There has never been any convincing evidence that mind-altering drugs increase human intellectual power, despite some popular belief to the contrary. Mind-altering drugs do, unquestionably, have a major affect on our emotions by suppressing the intellect. The crying or jovial drunk and the angry and homicidal cocaine addict, are examples of this. There is also indisputable evidence that mind-altering drugs "lower our inhibitions" — relax our ethical standard — leading to a shift toward more overt and sometimes destructive animal behavior. Some mind-altering drugs also affect perception resulting in a distorted interpretation of events.

Although the use of mind-altering drugs is associated with the animal side of our nature, experience has shown that at least one, alcohol, can be used by many people in a way that provides pleasure without harm. However, this is a potentially dangerous activity. A major problem is that mind-altering drugs, including alcohol, are frequently abused in ways that are very destructive. The knowing use of mind-altering drugs in ways that can be expected to produce reckless and destructive behavior makes one an animal. So does the production and sale of mind-altering drugs under circumstances that promote destructive behavior.

Emotional Character of Drug Addiction

Persons who have developed true addiction to mind-altering drugs have lost the capacity to control behavior. Such persons cannot be held to an ethical standard until their addiction is cured by effective treatment. Drug addiction has strong similarities to an emotional state like love. Drugs may produce a physical craving based on biological dependency, but they also result in a powerful emotional feeling similar to love – *love for the drug*. Addicts will not stop using a drug even though it is obvious to them and others that it is killing them. Once established, this emotional attachment to the drug is hardwired and refractory to intellectual pleading and logic just like other forms of emotion. Some addictions can be reversed by forms of treatment employing emotion such as religious and group psychotherapy, as with Alcoholics Anonymous or with formal *interventions* in the form of organized confrontations by a group of loved ones.

Bureaucracy

I was only following orders

Bureaucracy

Bureaucracy is commonly thought of as a characteristically human invention. What is more typical of modern society than bureaucracy? But bureaucratic activity began well before emergence of the human side of our intellect. Bureaucracy built the pyramids of ancient Egypt and Mexico and bureaucracy ran ancient dynasties in India and China. The extent of the influence of bureaucracy in contemporary life is almost inconceivable. Bureaucracy runs all governments, corporations, and universities of the world as well as most other organized human activities in which groups of people are engaged in work. Bureaucracy is all pervasive.

What Is Bureaucracy?

Besides its obvious effectiveness in "getting things done," the question can be asked - "does bureaucracy have any other purpose and does it affect our lives in other ways?" Also, where did bureaucracy come from and how does it fit into our human development? The answer to these questions is surprisingly simple although we appear to be oblivious to it.

Originated in Dominance

The answer is that bureaucracy is nothing more than the living, breathing, continuation of our animal striving for *dominance*. Our dominance-seeking behavior probably began when we were in an early evolutionary stage and certainly existed during our early humanoid and human phases. Nobody invented bureaucracy, it just evolved with us. It has undergone cultural changes like all human activities.

Cultural Adaptations Have Occurred

The basic rule of "the game" is still the same. You are ranked according to your position on the dominance scale of your organization. Most dominant will get you the CEO/President position; least dominant, and you are in some unpleasant location doing something not very interesting and wondering when the "pink slip" will arrive. Also, the object of the game is still the same, *to get to the top.*

But the rules governing the ways in which this can be accomplished have been brought up-to-date. Being the best at physically fighting and bluffing are no longer the essential qualities needed to reach the top, although being a "fighter" can still be important. Under the new rules you can also get to the top if you are very smart and made good decisions that earn your company a lot of money or if your skill in organizing the operation leads to success.

Otherwise, the rules have not changed; you may dominate all those who are lower-ranked than you, which includes your having a bigger office and better furnishings than they. But, you must be prepared to submit to domination by all of those above you on the scale. Also, you should show no signs of weakness and avoid admitting any errors, especially to those below you on the dominance scale. Never apologizing unless absolutely necessary is part of this same animal strategy, since to show weakness is to invite attack.

A benefit from your position in a bureaucracy is that the ultimate responsibility for events is not your concern or responsibility, unless you happen to be number one. You can "pass the buck" – avoid responsibility for your actions. As long as you meet the approval of your superiors, you can turn on your voice mail and not return telephone calls, be rude to anybody you believe cannot threaten your position, and hold up the work of other people by not meeting their needs in a timely way – all very satisfying to your vanity. *Vanity, of course, is a major part of the dominance game in addition to actual authority.*

Dangers of Bureaucracy

All of this is to say that bureaucracy, as it exists today, is clearly not just about organizing people so that work can be accomplished in an effective manner, it is also very much about dominance, vanity, responsibility, and irresponsibility in interpersonal relations. Dominance is one of the most powerful forces that affects human behavior along with biological needs and emotion. As has been shown by observations of chimpanzees and other animal species, once an individual's rank is established in a dominance hierarchy, there is a strong tendency for that individual to remain submissive to superiors in the hierarchy, "the authorities," so to speak. And that leads to the dark side of bureaucracy and to the unspeakable horrors with which it has been associated.

Documents are available concerning some of the worst examples of the concentration camps of recent times. These contain numerous testimonials that the people carrying out these programs of wholesale human extermination were often of "average normality." Although sadists and other mentally deranged persons were involved at times, the mind numbing discovery was made that the death camps were often run by quite ordinary people. These manufacturers of wholesale atrocity and murder, these marketers of a holocaust, were not political fanatics nor individuals who had been hardened by rigorous psychological conditioning, although some existed. Many were simply doing a job, obeying orders from their superiors, and, thus, "avoiding" personal responsibility for their actions. This is an extreme example of the destructive potential of bureaucracy and to be sure the environment of unrestrained terror of totalitarianism was a powerful force in overcoming conscience.

Less dramatic examples of the destructive power of bureaucracy occur all the time. Individuals in all types of bureaucracies lie or engage in other forms of dishonest or uncaring behavior for "the good of the organization" or because they are "just following orders" and feel no sense of responsibility for their behavior. If you work in a bureaucracy, and in dealing with people, you avoid following Ethic because of bureaucratic rules and regulations, you are behaving like an animal. You are not using your own conscience to direct your behavior.

Pathological Domination

Thus, bureaucracy serves the dual functions of aiding productivity and of continuing the practice of dominance in an organized fashion. The philosopher, Hannah Arendt, analyzed the reasons for what appeared, on the surface, to be an irrational waste of human resources – slave labor – in the concentration camps. She concluded that the potential productivity of a slave labor force was deliberately ignored in order to exploit the camp's main role, a mechanism for *domination*. She persuasively argues that the real purpose of the camps was the total domination of the residents in the most complete way imaginable. In her opinion, the camps were an unprecedented example of dominance-seeking behavior run amuck, conceived by the intellect of persons whose goal was to ultimately dominate every single person on the planet. All the reasons for the holocaust may never be understood and all the mechanics identified but, bureaucracy in its most destructive form was a major part of the workings of this monstrous aberration. Is it any wonder then that in this book, bureaucracy along with mental illness, mind-altering drugs, entertainment and the arts, and fashion is placed among the threats to the ethical integrity of the human intellect?

Entertainment and the Arts

He who laughs, leads

Anonymous, undated

Entertainment and the Arts

One of our most conspicuous characteristics as a species is that we spend large amounts of our time being entertained. Entertainment and the arts are a major force in most people's lives. Our most popular entertainments aside from social activity are currently television, movies, and computer networks. In our current existence, hundreds of millions of people around the world spend large amounts of time daily watching television. Before that, it was radio, stage performances, reading, games, music, and story-telling. This is not to say that contemporary humans do not continue to engage in all of these forms of entertainment at one time or another.

Animal Origins

What is the nature of these activities we seek so avidly? Entertainment and art are very old activities for us, so that it is not surprising that they have an emotional content, and that subject matter is mainly devoted to our animal interests. Whether on an informal level through conversation and other social interactions or with professional entertainment, our most common and entertaining topics are gossip about other people and stories involving violence, fighting, loving, sex, and adventure.

Intellectual and Ethical Content Secondary

The success of entertainment comes from the skill with which the entertainer achieves a vivid and moving production which stirs our *emotions* – not our intellects. The intellectual content of entertainment is important only in that it should be appropriate for the intelligence of the audience. The ethical content of entertainment is also irrelevant to its success as long as it also is not overly offensive to the ethical standards of the audience to whom it is directed.

Abuses

With entertainment and art being primarily directed at our emotions, it is not surprising that it is easily subjected to abuse. Entertainment and art can be and are used for destructive purposes in several ways. They may be destructive because they convey an unethical message – lying, stealing, and assaulting are presented as acceptable and fashionable behavior. Also, some people have become very skilled at improperly using entertainment to sell their products, promote their ideas, and even to help fight their wars. With emotion often leading to action, the story of the opera, *La Muette De Poritici*, stirring the emotions of the audience to such a fevered pitch that they rushed out of the opera house and started a revolution is entirely understandable. Entertainment and art are used improperly when the commercial or ideological message is deliberately hidden in the content in such a way that the recipient is not aware of being influenced. Commercials and other persuasive ideas are not unethical when used openly in association with entertainment, but when skillfully incorporated into the entertainment itself, they are a cause for concern.

Power Over Intellect

The problem we face in using entertainment and art wisely is that its emotional power subverts our intellect, leading us to believe and do things that may be harmful to ourselves and others. It has been said that at the present time some people do not believe something has actually happened or is true unless they see it on television. The artificial medium has become so powerful that it overcomes the real life message received through the senses or personally experienced. Successful public speakers and entertainers know that as they tell their stories or present their messages, if they can get their audience to laugh or cry with them, the audience will be more likely to accept the ideas they wish to convey. This is especially true if they are presenting material which supports the preexisting hopes of their audience or strengthens their preexisting denial. Therefore, skillfully delivered emotional content is a very important, if not essential, part of rhetoric, especially when it contains appeals to fear, anger, hope, denial, and prejudice. Throughout history, demagogues and tyrants have used this well known – to them – technique to gain control over our emotions and, thus, control our intellects. It is somewhat amazing – and a tribute to the skill of such people – that they continue to hold power over us through this means and that most of us continue to fall for their schemes. This ability to delude has been especially useful for charismatic leaders who use their ability to make emotional contact to cover up their dishonest, corrupt, and tyrannical actions.

Francisco Goya

Entertainment and the arts do not always serve destructive purposes. They have also been a powerful force for enlightenment by expanding self-awareness. Francisco Goya requires special recognition for the unflinching look at ourselves which we receive through his art. After many years of painting scenes of life in Spain and portraits of the rich and powerful, he turned to follow his genius by creating an art of "human" revelation that has no equal. This work, the paintings of his "Black Period" and his etchings of "The Disasters of War," and of "Los Caprichos" show our continuing potential for destructive and degrading animal behavior.

In the work, "human" features are coarsened and distorted and appear as they would in anatomical drawings in which the skin has been stripped from the face – he shows us ourselves beneath the surface. "Human" actions of brutality, depravity, and senseless violence are shown in exquisitely revolting and painful detail. Through the power of his intellect and the genius of his art, Goya tears away the vanity and denial which filter out the reality of our shameful animal behavior and help support the myth of our human purity. His graphic dehumanization of people is as exquisite as it is powerful – the proof of its success our revulsion and shame. Goya's commentary is on all of us, rich and poor, powerful and weak, intelligent and dull, religious and irreligious; he played no favorites because he saw us at a level where such things are irrelevant. As Goya himself said "Divine reason, do not spare anyone."

Standing in a darkened gallery in the Prado Museum surrounded by the somber paintings of his Black Period, you watch subdued people pass through the room with impassive faces and whispered comments. No seats are provided in the room and none appear to be needed; most do not stay long. Body language speaks of distaste, anxiety, and fear. And, truly, the scenes in the paintings are black in mood, frightening, and painful to behold. And yet, in the reality of Goya's intellectual genius, the room is suddenly filled with a pure and brilliant light, as are few places on this earth. His work illuminates a message of such power, that when understood, a feeling arises of freedom and space. An invigoration occurs as though one is breathing a fresh and pure mountain breeze. This man is telling us the truth about ourselves! A close and darkened room becomes a mountain peak bathed by the brilliant unfiltered sunlight of human understanding and washed by the jet stream of human truth. This is not madness but sublime truth.

Such are the "black" works of Francisco Goya, and such his contribution to our awareness of the potential for unlimited animal brutality and depravity that resides within us. Goya provides a visual masterpiece that is a noble and fitting companion to the literary masterpiece on this subject by Hannah Arendt.

Ethical Responsibility

Because of its potential for leading to destructive behavior and causing harm, it is logical that the content of entertainment and art should be judged by the standards applied to other important human activities. Entertainment can develop such a powerful hold on our emotions and on our animal "pleasure center" that it appears to be capable of leading to an addiction similar to mind-altering drugs. The term "television addict" may in fact be an accurate description of a true addiction which may affect some persons. Judging entertainment and art is not meant to imply that external censorship should be applied. What it does mean is that persons engaged in these activities should pass judgement on themselves and the content of their material. Persons who knowingly supply entertainment which subverts Ethic, and persons knowingly watching such entertainment should recognize the pure animal state in which they are.

Fashion

Quite out of fashion, like a rusty mail
in monumental mockery

Shakespeare, 400 years ago
(4,999,600 HO)

Show me the clothes

Fashion

Fashion is a very powerful force in our lives – fashion as it relates not only to personal appearance and clothing but also fashion in other things like foods and entertainment; even fashion in philosophic, religious, and scientific beliefs. We want to be fashionable, and we are ashamed when we are thought to be unfashionable. This goes far back into our animal roots – as part of our "herd mentality" – and is related to our concern for dominance. Part of success in dominating depends on presenting a proper – fashionable – appearance.

Concern with personal fashion in the form of tattooing and adornment existed in the upper Paleolithic period which began 50 thousand years ago. Even the poor Neanderthals, before they became extent, appeared to have made crude personal ornaments. Its animal origin explains why concern with fashion has strong emotional connections, why it pervades our thinking and behavior, and why it can override our intellect. We fear that being out of fashion will bring the shame of "monumental mockery" described by Shakespeare.

Being fashionable is part of our normal healthy animal behavior, but it has no relationship to being human. It is irrelevant to the practice of Ethic. Like other emotionally driven forces which affect our behavior, it can be destructive. If we are obsessed with being fashionable and this leads to uncaring and illogical behavior which is harmful to others, we are obviously behaving like animals, not humans. If we judge the worth of other people on the basis of how fashionable they are rather than on their ethical behavior, we are also missing the human mark. Finally, believing in an idea which is based on fashion – the prevailing opinion of admired "experts" – and not on the evidence, is a well established danger which continues to trick our intellects. This also is an animal way of thinking.

WAYS THE INTELLECT IS MISLED

There is a sucker born every minute

P.T. Barnum, 150 years ago
(9,999,850 HO)

Ways the Intellect Is Misled

Did it ever occur to you that there are many ways to mislead the intellect? To trick your intellect? There are ways to trick the intellect and it happens to us every day. This was recognized by the showman, P.T. Barnum, in his famous quotation which introduces this section.

Lying

Of course there are lies, lots of lies. Rudyard Kipling thought it wasn't even worth worrying about the lies. In one of his novels, he said that "life was too short to keep track of every lie along the coast." Lying works in the short-term, but lies of any consequence are usually found out eventually. Of course, in the short-term, lies can do great harm. Lying is particularly effective when it is done on a grand scale. Big lies, huge lies, especially when spoken by people with the trappings of authority, are very believable. This works because people with normal intellects reason that "who would believe" anybody in "that position" could be such a monumental and open liar. By the *human* standard of Ethic, it does not make sense and, in fact, it turns out that these kinds of liars often are intellectually impaired in some way. Their intellects are sick, or perhaps they are only normal people whose intellectual development is still in the pure animal stage – they have no conscience – and are thus incapable of practicing Ethic.

"Negative" lies, not telling the whole story, are also very effective. The difficulty that our intellects have with recognizing "nothing," the absence of something, has been discussed. So if you hear only part of the story, it is difficult to realize that you have not heard the rest of the story. And the rest of the story may reveal the lie.

And what about the little white lies about someone's taste in clothes, cooking, or choice of art. We are all part animal and the truth about these things can be painful. But our human side – if we have one – wants to know the truth. With the personal standard of humans being Ethic and not dominance — getting ahead of our neighbors — these things are not of the most importance. Also, we can improve in our performance in material things only when we do know the truth about ourselves.

Lying to Yourself

Of perhaps the greatest importance of all is lying to yourself. Without being honest with yourself, you will fool your intellect just as surely as another who lies to you. This is perhaps the most frequent and important way that our intellects are misled. We do it by denying — suppressing — ideas we find unpleasant and through hypocrisy — saying one thing and doing another. Sometimes this occurs at a subconscious level, but often in our heart of hearts we know what we are doing. We arrive at illogical — animal — conclusions to justify our behavior. Remember, *logic is an intellectual accomplishment of humans only.*

While we cannot always avoid animal behavior which is destructive, we should at least try to admit to ourselves that by engaging in this behavior we are being animals. By exercising honest, logical self-judgement in these situations, we are at least starting on the path to human behavior.

Did it Ever
Occur to You
That ...

"Balance" is not a substitute for "truth"

Seeking Balance

The idea of presenting a "balanced point of view" is very appealing and popular because it sounds enlightened and "fair." But balance is not a substitute for truth. In discussing the shape of the earth, it would be absurd to balance the views of those who say it is flat against those who believe it is round. For uninformed individuals who are planning a world tour, this would have serious consequences for their itinerary. This you say is a silly example, but it is not. The reason you say the example is ridiculous is because you *know* the world is round. But the chances are you *don't know* about the important characteristics of a new medical treatment you might be told to use or of new products you might be encouraged to buy. Do you want the equivalent of the "flat earth" view on such things as this given equal weight to established facts? And there really are established facts. The world really is round and not flat. And some new medical treatments really work and some do not. And some new products have value and some do not.

How Balance Misleads

Thomas Jefferson, in dedicating the University of Virginia, said "For here we are not afraid to follow the truth, wherever it may lead, nor to tolerate any error so long as reason is left free to combat it." The advice he was giving was not to seek *balance* but by examining different points of view, to try to find *truth*. The problem with "balancing" ideas is that ideas have different degrees of truthfulness – validity. Some ideas are based on the empiricism of scientific study, some are based on long and frequent experience, some on a single experience, some on an unproven theory, some on an emotional belief, some on spiritual faith, and some on outright lies. Thus, they have very different weights. This obviously presents a problem to the balancing approach. Without accurate information on the relative validity of conflicting ideas, it is not possible to correctly judge their "weight."

Some Ideas Cannot Be Weighed

In the first place, there is no way to "weigh" the validity of an idea which is based on spiritual faith or emotional belief. To speak of balancing these kinds of beliefs and value judgements make no sense. When someone claims to be balancing the intellectual content of spiritual faith or emotional belief, be wary. The best they can measure and balance is the *emotional intensity* of the belief or faith. Such an activity has no *intellectual* substance which can be measured. As discussed earlier, faith is based on emotion and cannot be measured against an intellectual standard.

How to Measure Intellectual Content

Therefore, to be a measurable idea, it must have intellectual content. What is the intellectual quality which is capable of being weighed? The quality being weighed is *how well the idea conforms to reality*; good conformation to reality gives a high weight and poor conformation to reality gives a low weight. Ideas based on controlled experimentation, in general, have more weight than those based on experience. And ideas based on experience in general have more weight than those based on "theory," which is a special category of belief or faith. Those based on deliberate misrepresentation obviously have no weight at all.

With this understanding, we can now return to the example of the "balance" of the "round earth" versus the "flat earth" ideas, a real historical controversy. The idea of the "round earth" is now obviously very, very heavy. It conforms to the reality of the observations made by early astronomers, to Christopher Columbus' experience in sailing to the new world, and that of your friend on her last trip around the world. It also conforms to the satellite pictures of the earth. On the other hand, the idea of "flat earth" has become pretty light. It was supported by the sincere *belief*, based on perceptual experience, of early people, now dead, and the "belief" of a few living eccentrics in the Flat Earth Society about whom we cannot help but wonder if they are "putting us on." If we put the ideas of "round earth" versus "flat earth" on the scale, they are totally out of balance unless the one doing the weighing adds artificial weight to the flat earth side, and that's the problem.

Misleading Presentations

When we are sanctimoniously told that we are being presented a "balanced view" of a question, we tend to assume there is some degree of equal weight to the conflicting ideas or why bother. But we rarely are given information that would help us determine the true weights of the conflicting ideas. We are not told on what the respective ideas are based – scientific testing, experience, theory, belief, faith, lies? Also, we are not usually informed about the quality of the testing or experience or even if such information exists. We are not told any of this crucial information so we cannot estimate the respective weights of the ideas. By not telling us this crucial information, and by implying that there is some balance between the ideas, the writer or commentator is, in fact, not giving us a true measure of their weights. They are adding artificial "weight" to the light weight idea. Such artificial weight may come in the form of untruths or partial truths or it can represent genuine ignorance about the subject or lack of understanding of the elements of causality. Thus, false weight may be created simply by implying that enough "balance" exists to raise a valid question about the issue. The "balancing" approach is a very effective way to fool the intellect because it has intellectual and emotional appeal. It sounds so good. And if there were not a real question at issue, why would "they" bother us about it in the first place?

Did it Ever
Occur to you
That ...

Romantic - means having no basis in fact

          Webster's Dictionary

Romanticism

Romanticism is a literary, artistic, and philosophical movement with an emphasis on the imagination and emotions. In so far as romanticism rests on the emotions, it cannot be considered as a product of the intellect, since as has been discussed earlier, feeling an emotion is not the same type of activity as having a thought. Romanticism has had a major effect on attitudes since its origination in the 18th century, and it continues to have a strong attraction. It is especially appealing to people who may be weary of the past or threatened by the present. As such, romanticism is a form of escapism or denial which can provide comfort to those seeking to avoid a world with ever increasing complexity and "stress". "I am going to let my feelings guide me." "I am going back to simple things and natural ways." An important element of romanticism is an exaltation of the primitive human – "the noble savage." In this, romanticism shows features of the idea expressed in the creation myth of the pure human.

While the literary and artistic components of romanticism have added to the beauty of human life, its adoption as a philosophy is anti-intellectual and can be harmful. Because it is based on feeling and emotion, romanticism originates from our animal being and not from the human part of the intellect. Also, because of its unhistorical belief in the purity of the early human, it leads to a misunderstanding of the true course of human intellectual maturation. It ignores the intellect's role in the development of Ethic and in an understanding of causation. Romanticism may result in the investment of material and spiritual capital in the wrong kinds of projects and goals. In so far as romanticism leads to a conscious abandonment of the control of behavior to the emotions, it represents a deliberate adoption of a purely animal form of life. As such, the intellectual capacity of the individual lies idle. There is no chance to understand causation or to practice Ethic.

Did it Ever
Occur to You
That ...

The pen is mightier
than the truth

Artificial Communication through the Media

A humorist named James Thurber once said "Don't get it right, get it written." What he meant by this was that written, broadcast, or televised ideas – forms of artificial communication – have an authority which is disproportionate to their truthfulness – confirmation to reality. This is part of the "big lie" phenomenon. "If that stuff was untrue or misleading *they* wouldn't write it, broadcast it, or televise it, would they?" You bet your life "they" would and do! A famous columnist likes to say "Wake up and smell the coffee." That is good advice here.

Animal Charisma

The people who produce, direct, and talk in the media are only people, but they are usually very smooth, clever, sophisticated, and often attractive. They have *lots* of animal charisma. *We love them*; we are strongly emotionally attached to them. Does that make your intellect vulnerable to trickery? And let me ask you what percent of these people believe in or follow Ethic? We do not know. We never get to meet them.

Manipulation of Material

The media also are in a position to manipulate the content of what is presented. With editing, this has always been true to a certain extent, but with modern technology such as taping and computer generation of images, there is a much greater opportunity for this activity. Targets of the media discover that their own words are manipulated by the media to give the media's message rather than their own. For this reason, live programming has less potential for abuse than that prepared from tapes.

Lack of Intellectual Interaction

The biggest problem with some of the most popular types of artificial communication is that they do not provide the opportunity for a timely interaction between the intellect of the sender and that of the receiver of the message (Table 3). The sender has the psychological advantage, not only of the authority associated with the technology of the delivery, but also with being in the position of escaping timely comments, questions, and criticisms from his or her listener. The sender's pronouncements, thus, share certain features of communication which have been attributed to divine messages from Omnipotent Powers. This type of one-way communication has also been successfully used by kings and tyrants throughout history.

With repeated exposure to messages delivered in an authoritative manner, and which are never subject to immediate correction or criticism, there is the danger that the intellect of the receiver will eventually be overwhelmed. This may result in the acceptance of ideas which are incorrect or destructive and which would not be accepted in the course of direct person-to-person communication. The media are very much about dominance. The media try to dominate us and very often do. That is one important reason members of the media show such strong reluctance to ever admit that they are "wrong" or have been in error – appearing infallible is important in establishing and maintaining dominance.

At best, the receiver of the media message has no opportunity to exercise his or her intellect in the free exchange of ideas. This has the potential for leading to intellectual stunting and atrophy. Although study in this area has shown there can be some resistance and resilience of the intellect to this type of assault, the obvious success of commercial advertising and political propaganda shows that it is very effective. The exorbitant cost of television advertising should be a clue to how effectively the media affects our thinking. Why are corporations and political candidates paying millions and millions of dollars to send us their messages in this way?

Table 3. Communication and the Availability of Intellectual Interaction

Types of Communication	Intellectual Interaction Available
Person-to-Person	yes
Writing	
personal letters	yes
newspapers	no*
magazines	no*
books	no
Telephone	yes
Radio	no*
Television	no*
Fax	yes
Electronic mail	yes
Internet	yes

*Only a very small proportion of persons receiving a message can interact through letters to the editors, telephone "call-in," etc.

Intellectual and Ethical Responsibility

Thus, the output of the media can be a major threat to intellectual integrity. This does not mean that these types of artificial communication should be abandoned. It does mean that people delivering a message in this way have both the intellectual responsibility to try to see that the message is as well researched and accurate as possible and the ethical responsibility to see that the message is presented in a truthful way. The latter responsibility includes delivering the full message and placing it in a context which accurately discloses its intended meaning. Will Rogers was an American humorist with a first-rate intellect and a commitment to Ethic. He once said "I try to know what I'm talking about. I joke to the public, but I do a lot of studying because, although I hand out a lot of foolishness, I don't want to hand out stuff that might be misleading." Good advice!

How to Defend Yourself

At one time very few people could write so it was natural to believe that those who could were smart and talented, which they usually were, and that what they wrote was important and true, which was not necessarily so. Now as then, the intellectual content of what is written, broadcast, or televised ultimately reflects the product of some real person's intellect. The truth of the idea and its value has nothing to do with the intimidating technology used for its delivery. You also have an intellect. Do not forget that. It is hoped you already understand Ethic if you have a conscience, and you can learn to understand causality if you do not already. Wake up your intellect so that it can smell the coffee, the roses, and the rotten eggs you are served every day by the media.

Did it Ever
Occur to You
That ...

Wisdom is character dependent; intelligence is not

Intelligence without Wisdom

We admire and are influenced by strong intellects, that is to say, intelligence. We want intelligent friends, and intelligent leaders, and, also, we hope that we ourselves are intelligent. This book is about the intellect, the capacity to think. Intellectual capacity separates us from the animals. But raw intelligence has its limits. *Raw intelligence is not the same as wisdom.* Acquiring wisdom requires more than intelligence; it requires character, having a set of values. Having character provides a reference point for developing enlightened experience and knowledge. This reference point allows us to "profit" from our experience and study, and that profit is the source of our wisdom. If experience is not incorporated into a stable frame-work of value, it has no permanent meaning and is lost. The philosopher Søren Kierkegaard understood this. He wrote "Events in the past do not determine the commitment I have, rather the commitment I have gives me an interpretation of the events of my past." The human commitment is Ethic. We support our human intellectual progress towards wisdom by believing and practicing Ethic. Without the support of Ethic, our intellect is without a foundation on which to grow and mature. We do not become wise.

Did it Ever
Occur to You
That ...

Utopian ideas block attainable progress

Utopian Paralysis of the Intellect

Ideals Are Not Attainable

Ideals are important for spiritual growth and maturation of human character and as a practical way of controlling our destructive behavior. There can be no question that without ideals we cannot attain full human development. However, it is important to remember that ideals by their very nature are never completely attainable. We must "do the best we can." Doing the best we can to reach our ideals because it is a uniquely human attitude, is vastly superior to having no ideals.

Danger of Perfectionism

But we also are biological beings and because of that, we are imperfect. A successful dog trainer put it this way, "One of the secrets of training is not trying for perfection; *a certain amount of tolerance is necessary.*" We can say the same thing about ourselves. We have to give ourselves and others a certain amount of tolerance. When the emotional or legalistic drive for perfection becomes excessive, the intellect is no longer able to function effectively. General George Patton of the American Army in World War II wrote that in planning for a battle, "The best is the enemy of the good." By this he meant it was important to develop a good – not perfect – battle plan and execute it promptly. Waiting to develop the "perfect" plan could lead to disaster if an important opportunity was lost.

Do It

Because of the fear of failure, with its powerful associated emotion of shame, we are susceptible to "utopian paralysis syndrome" in which, unless something can be done perfectly, we do not want to do "it." This is another type of emotional trap we lay for our intellect. This is also a trick other people play on us to stop us from doing something they do not want us to do. These obstructions are often presented in the form of pre-conditions which prior experience has shown are impractical or as dogmatic criticisms which are made in the absence of alternative solutions. The latter is an illogical way of thinking commonly used. While it is important to point out unrecognized or dangerous features of a plan, having done this, to continue to focus on them when faced with a situation in which there is agreement that action is needed, accomplishes no useful purpose. All actions have both positive and negative consequences under certain circumstances, and the best we can ever do is to weigh all the known consequences with this understanding and then proceed or not. To insist that any activity or project be totally risk free is an illogical – animal – way of thinking.

Also, our increasingly legalistic society – where the letter of the law surpasses the spirit of the law in importance – imposes unrealistic constraints on our projects. The solution is not to forsake ideals but to recognize that they are never completely attainable. After adequate preparation, we must go on and begin our projects. The first step is usually the hardest because we must not only overcome the inertia inherent in a new activity but also the mental road blocks we put in our own path. We need to have the courage to overcome these obstacles and begin. Work can be made on improvements as we go along. The final judgement of quality should be made after the activity is completed. Also, it is often possible to make future improvements if necessary. We should not make intellectually paralyzing judgements before we start, and we should not listen to those of others.

AND FINALLY,
Did it Ever
Occur to You
That ...

You may be wrong

Inadequate Self-Evaluation

Openness to Criticism

Oliver Cromwell put it colorfully, "I beseech you in the bowels of Christ think it possible you may be mistaken." He presumably was addressing this remark to himself as well as to others. George Washington's intellect had a remarkable capacity for self-evaluation. He was more dignified when he said "I can bear to hear of imputed or real errors. The man, who wishes to stand well in the opinion of others, must do this because he is thereby enabled to correct his faults." Being able to start and complete projects in our lives is very important but accurately judging our own ideas and performance on these projects is also essential.

Animal Origin

Being emotionally unable to evaluate our own ideas and behavior is a very old problem for us. There are intelligent apes who will put their hand into a bottle to get a piece of fruit, and having grasped the fruit, find themselves unable to release their grip. Because of the narrow neck of the bottle, they are unable to remove their hand. Now, if the bottle is chained to a tree, which it is, since it is a type of trap, they are caught. It would seem that an intelligent ape would evaluate its idea of getting an easy meal, decide it was a bad idea, let go of the fruit, and escape capture. But it cannot. Emotion is too strong. Emotion has prevented self-analysis. Emotion has overcome intellect. Welcome to the zoo.

A Continuing Problem

We do the same thing to our intellect. Our strong animal emotions prevent the introspection necessary to examine the quality of our human ideas. It is often not that we don't have the intellectual competence to make the correct decisions before or after we get into trouble. But once aroused, our appetites and emotions never give our intellect a chance. Like the ape, the adrenalin and its hardwired response win again over our intellect, and we are trapped. The trap is more sophisticated than a piece of fruit in a jar. It may be a phoney investment, a quack medical cure, a real estate "deal," or a destructive personal belief but it works the same way. On an interpersonal level, the trap may be a prejudice we carry against some race, religion, or philosophical belief. And we, like the ape, not only get caught but often cannot let go, making matters worse.

SPIRITUALITY AND FAITH

Spirituality

We look at it and do not see it;
Its name is The Invisible
We listen to it and do not hear it;
Its name is The Inaudible.
We touch it and do not find it;
Its name is The Formless

>Lao Tzu, 2600 years ago
>(4,997,400 HO)

Spirituality

Human Knowledge of Self-Mortality

An event of great importance for our species was the development of spirituality. The origin of human spirituality is unclear, but it is reasonable to believe that it was influenced in part by the awareness of our own individual mortality, another manifestation of our intellectual self-awareness. This knowledge of inevitable death, which appears to be uniquely human, was given importance by early humans.

An African tribal legend which was told to Beryl Markham, the writer, goes as follows.."When the first man was made, he wandered alone in the great forest and on the plains, and he worried very much because he could not remember yesterday and so he could not imagine tomorrow. God saw this, so he sent the Chameleon to the first man with a message, saying that there would never be such a thing as death and that tomorrow would be like today, and that the days would never stop."

"Long after the Chameleon had started, God sent an Egret with a different message, saying that there would be a thing called Death and that, sometime, tomorrow would not come. 'Whichever message comes first to the ears of man,' God warned, 'will be the true one.'

"Now the Chameleon is a lazy animal. He thinks of nothing but food, and he moves only his tongue to get that. He lagged so much along the way that he arrived at the feet of the first man only a moment before the Egret."

"The Chameleon began to talk, but he could not. In the excitement of trying to deliver his tidings of eternal life, the Chameleon could only stutter and change, stupidly, from one colour to another. So the Egret, in a calm voice, gave the message of Death."

"Since then all men have died. Our people know this fact."

Leads to Introspection

Knowledge of the inevitability of death, death of loved ones and personal death is always a powerful cause of emotion and introspection. So powerful that on a day-by-day basis we avoid its knowledge by the use of denial. In the history of Buddhism, it is recounted that the young Buddha entered a life of religious contemplation and teaching after being made aware of his own mortality. Stories of similar spiritual awakening associated with recognition of the mortal state are very common and appear to have played an important role in our spiritual development.

Whatever the cause, affairs of the spirit as expressed in religious practice and belief in the supernatural are our oldest intellectual activity not directly related to biological needs for survival. The spirituality of humans is so ancient and powerful that its origins must relate to an important early intellectual turning point in our development as a species.

Lack of Awareness in Animals and Early Origins in Humans

The primitive recognition of death by animals is well documented. There are stories of death watches over loved ones by grieving elephants who have lost relatives and faithful dogs who have lost masters. These animal mourners, however, are not equipped with the self-awareness that allows them to relate these painful incidents to such an impending event in their own future.

The beginning crude spirituality of our ancestors, reflected in the adoption of burial rites, suggests that at that time, we were developing sufficient self-awareness to recognize our own mortality, although still lacking the intellectual capacity for fully developed self-judgement and an understanding of Ethic. The absence of archeological evidence of ritual burials before that time could indicate that a critical stage of self-awareness had just appeared. That self-awareness and its consequences can exist in different stages of development is shown by the fact that the higher primates are capable of self-recognition in a mirror but do have the intellectual capacity which has led us to Ethic and science. At the present time, most humans have some understanding of the principle of Ethic but relatively few understand the principles of causality on which contemporary science is based. The different rates of acquisition of these concepts is most likely cultural and not due to an increase in intellectual capacity. Our Cro-Magnon ancestor had a brain which anatomically appears to have been essentially the same as our own.

Limits to Determining Causation Define Spirituality and Faith

Much of religious and philosophical thinking over the past 3000 years shows a lack of understanding of causality and, more importantly, *a lack of understanding of the limits to the understanding of causation*. The interminable debates over such things as the nature of "existence" and "non-existence" and "reality" and "non-reality" are examples of addressing non-testable questions. Such thinking, while in some aspects "human" – since animals do not philosophize at all – is in reality a highly sophisticated residual of an animalistic level of understanding. Human understanding of causality at its most advanced level has led to the realization that causation can only be determined in matters that are testable – unless one is the beneficiary of divine revelation. The nature of "existence" is an example of a non-testable question. As discussed earlier, *non-testable beliefs are important, but they fall into the areas of philosophy and religion*. By their nature, these matters belong in the realm of *faith*. There is no logical or scientific – intellectual – way to arrive at the truth of ideas which are not testable. We must accept or reject such ideas on the basis of faith alone. The importance of this insight to you is that preoccupation with understanding – on an intellectual level – the "truth" of matters which cannot be tested can become a trap which diverts your intellect from more beneficial activity. Do not assign a task to your intellect that it is incapable of performing.

Faith

Faith is the substance of things hoped for, the evidence of things not seen

Saint Paul, 2000 years ago
(4,998,000 HO)

Faith

Emotional Origin

Faith is a product of our emotion given content and form by our intellect. Faith is part of the psychological mechanism which gives us our positive feelings about life. Healthy minds have a natural optimism that despite setbacks and troubles, "everything will turn out all right." This keeps us going in our everyday lives. Conscious faith appeared as part of our emerging human intellectual development, adding a new feature to our underlying animal positivism.

Faith has special significance in a religious context but faith is not exclusively religious in nature — people have faith in many things. Because faith is part of a very strong, positive emotion, it is really a special form of love; Jesus said..."God is love." The intellect alone cannot create faith. Rational "belief" has never worked. But the intellect does shape the character of faith. The origin of our faith is our animal nature, the reservoir of our emotions.

The emotional — animal — source of faith explains why early religious faith had such an animalistic character employing human sacrifice and cannibalism. These primitive religions arose before our intellect had conceived of the ideal of Ethic. When that did occur, Ethic, the new and superior way of thinking, was incorporated into religious belief. This is when the ethical religions first appear in history.

The Durability of Faith
Reflects Its Emotional Nature

Because of its emotional nature and its history of varied, even atrocious, intellectual content, religious faith may be difficult to acquire or even be scorned by some persons with a highly rational intellect. Also, some persons may place their faith in such non-intellectual concepts as magic, witchcraft, and astrology. But by the same token, because of its emotional origin, faith is also hard to destroy. This was shown by the great natural experiment of atheistic communism where decades of ruthless suppression could not exterminate religious faith.

Faith Has No Ethical Imperative

Faith remains contemporary by incorporating new ideas which are conceived by the intellect. This characteristic of faith produces the somewhat surprising paradox that "faith" per se has no ethical imperative. Depending on the current dogma it has adopted, it can be a strong constructive force as witnessed by the Christian faith's effect on the Roman Empire or a destructive forces as witnessed by its role in the Spanish Inquisition.

Holding Faith to the Standard of Ethic

Understanding this apparent paradox explains the mistake of believing that all religious beliefs and practices are constructive because they are part of a religious faith. Religions and other types of faith are constructive only so far as they incorporate and practice Ethic – truth telling, honesty, and concern for others. Because faith is so effective in influencing human behavior, its content should not be immune from judgement. Indeed, that is all the more reason that faith should be held to the standard of Ethic. Also, it is important to recognize that religions and other faith-based practices which contain obscure, mystical, and nonsensical beliefs can be a way of avoiding Ethic in our personal life. This kind of thinking can be an effective aid to the denial we use when we do not want to face our human conscience. "I must be a good person. After all, I am religious. I just want to do it my own way." Great lasting religions of both the East and the West incorporate the principle of Ethic. If you wish to adhere to a faith which does not incorporate Ethic, that is not a problem as long as the religion does not violate Ethic and as long as you also incorporate Ethic into your personal life. Otherwise, you may be fooling yourself about the ethical character of your spiritual and religious thinking and behavior.

Justification for Passing Judgement on Faiths

Religious freedom is an important principle but it has ethical limits when it leads to destructive behavior which harms people. The question may be asked, "Who are *we* to judge the sincere religious belief and practice of people different from us?" The answer is, we are *humans* equipped with the standard of Ethic. Having this standard enables us to recognize when behavior is destructive and damaging and when it is positive and uplifting. We have the ethical imperative to use this knowledge. Critics of this answer may say that the persons directing the Spanish Inquisition may have had the same certainty and "fanaticism," and that they would have given the same answer to the question. The reply to that criticism is that the religious roots of the Spanish Inquisition had to do with forcibly "saving souls" by combating perceived heresy. The persons directing the Inquisition were definitely not practicing Ethic. Ethic says nothing about forcibly changing other peoples beliefs and behavior. In no stretch of the imagination would the kind of unrestrained physical and emotional torture that was practiced in the Inquisition come under the practice of Ethic. Ethic leaves salvation up to the individual. Ethic is concerned with *your own behavior*, not that of other people.

Myth and Reality

To know good and evil

Genesis, 2500 years ago
(4,997,500 HO)

Myth and Reality

This book describes the same event — human self-recognition — which is told in the story of Adam and Eve. It is about the same subject, the intellectual and spiritual development which followed that self-recognition. After Eve and Adam ate the forbidden fruit, "the eyes of them both were opened and they knew they were naked and they became ashamed," and through their self-awareness, they came "to know good and evil." Thus, they acquired a powerful new emotion, *shame*, and a transforming addition to their intellect, *the power of self-judgement*, the development of a conscience. In the experience of our real human ancestors, which is recounted in this book, self-recognition had similar results. Self-recognition led to the capacity for experiencing shame and to the capacity for self-judgement. Self-judgement resulted in understanding the importance of Ethic as a standard of behavior.

The story of the self-awakening of Adam and Eve is told with great spiritual inspiration in the first three chapters of the first book of the Judeo-Christian Bible. Our own story, which is known to us through archeological, anthropological, historical, and now, molecular evidence, suggests that we also are in an early stage of self-awareness. As true humans, we are as new to the world as Adam and Eve. The one major difference between the story of Adam and Eve and the current message is the interpretation given to the significance of self-awareness. In *Genesis*, developing the capacity for self-awareness and self-judgement is said to have made innocent beings created "in the image of God" into cognizant humans. In the reality of anthropological discovery described in this book, developing the capacity for self-awareness and self-judgement changed *homo sapiens* from brute animals into humans! As such, self-recognition has been the most elevating event in our development — giving us a conscience and a unique ability to understand causation.

I have characterized the author of *Genesis* as possessed of "spiritual" inspiration. However, millions of people have recognized a higher dimension to the origin of Genesis and have attributed it to "divine" inspiration. Because faith by its nature is not subject to logical analysis, who is to say they are wrong? If material proof could be obtained of the existence of an Omnipotent Power, there would be no need for faith; in fact, the concept of faith would have no meaning. But as humans who can never attain true cosmic understanding in this life, each of us alone has the privilege and responsibility for our own spiritual and religious beliefs.

CONCLUSION

Summary

The present generation is ignorant
about human nature

Tung Chung-shu, 2100 years ago
(4,997,900 HO)

Summary

When will it be possible for us to know and understand what we humans truly are? To know ourselves with the fullness and honesty of which our intellectual capacity is capable and deserves? This book is written in the belief that the time has come.

There is very little mystery in "human" nature, in "human" behavior. Once you are able to rid your own mind of its belief in the creation myth of human purity – not an easy task – our nature is as plain as day. We are a lot of animal and a little bit of human. As animals, we carry out our daily activities, as animals we work and play, as animals we love and hate, as animals we fight and form friendships, and as animals we build and destroy. This routine is *sometimes* influenced by our human conscience, our human self-judgement, our human reason, but often it is not. Our feeble human intellect struggles weakly with our powerful animal needs and emotions. It is a hard struggle – when we make the effort. Often, we do not even try. We do "bad" things to other people. This is not hard to understand. Animals naturally do "bad" things to other animals. We – when our animal nature is in control – do the same to each other. What is the mystery? There is none.

Two discoveries have been made in our time which tell the human story with great force and clarity. One, a description of the behavioral pattern of our near animal relative, the chimpanzee, is based on simple, but ingenious observations in the field. The other, the disclosure of the very close genetic relatedness of humans and the higher primates, is based on sophisticated molecular biology. The two discoveries, when viewed together, provide indisputable evidence for our origins and a clear and forceful explanation for our organic behavior. To know and to understand the implications of these discoveries is to know our true biological selves. With this knowledge, we can then understand our emergence as humans.

The chimpanzee studies have been done, and the lesson is plainly there to see – primitive primate behavior in chimpanzees and a continuation, with cultural modifications, of the same behavior in ourselves. The similarities are too obvious for chance; the parallels too powerful to dispute.

The core patterns of chimpanzee social behavior are basically very simple. Chimpanzee social behavior has two major themes, striving for dominance within groups and aggressive and violent behavior over territorial boundaries among groups. Both males and females strive for intra-group dominance, with males having dominance over females. Both threats and physical force are used in the intra-group competition, but assaults are usually restrained and serious injury mostly avoided. Individuals in dominant positions enjoy privileges in food selection and mating, and dominant males carry responsibilities for leadership in territorial surveillance and defense. With the inter-group rivalries over territorial boundaries, the level of violence is unrestrained and this simian warfare often leads to serious injury and death.

Parallels in human behavior are obvious enough, although our behavior is more subtle and often masked or modified by cultural devices. Striving for dominance among our peers remains at the core of our own bureaucratic behavior with remarkably little difference from that of the chimpanzee. Unrestrained aggression and violent behavior over territorial domains, what we call war, has provided the main theme of our history. For both species, territorial control has been an historical imperative for insuring a supply of the essentials for life, mainly food. For the chimpanzee, this is still true, and a chimpanzee band which loses too much of its territory is doomed to extinction.

Males of our own species have historically striven for dominance over other males and have dominated females, using both threats of force and restrained physical force. In early versions of the marriage ceremony, the woman was instructed to *obey* the man, thus, providing a means for reducing the physical force employed in male-female relationships. Gradual changes in our male-female relationship are continuing to occur as the result of cultural development, but the basic pattern of this biological behavior is still intact.

These similarities in the core behaviors of the two species confirm the animal side of our human character, but they are not an accurate indication of the large intellectual and spiritual difference between apes and humans. Quantification of the magnitude of these differences is, of course, a human judgement, but human standards are the only standards. For those who may say this knowledge dehumanizes us and for others who may say this information proves the lower species are our equals, I can only say that both are wrong. We are uniquely what we are. An intellect has emerged in our being which is an essential part of the human condition and of no other on this planet. Our failings are many, our strivings often weak, our behavior frequently despicable, but we alone are capable of self-judgement, we alone have an ethical ideal, and we alone control the awesome power of science. Through science, we now control nucleic acid and through nucleic acid, we now control all life on earth in its most basic and vulnerable form. With our unique human intellect, we have dominated a planet. Such as we are, we are the best there is and the worst there is, and as such we are the undisputed rulers of the world. We rule because of what we are. Both our actions and our failure to take action have global consequences. We have no choice but to rule.

Biological being is programmed by chemical molecules, and our own molecule reflects the history of our past. We emerged in the great primate family, great because of its intellectual power. The members of that family are our closest chemical kin. So close that the composition of our own determinative molecule is almost identical to the composition of the determinative molecule of our primate cousins. This knowledge is difficult to comprehend. We know the difference between ourselves and the apes! We keep them for pets and look at them in zoos. Our shame and vanity shape our views and cause our inability to fully accept the truth of our relatedness. But we must profit from this knowledge. It provides an invaluable opportunity to view a species of almost like identity to ourselves which is far different from us in intellectual and spiritual development. We have an opportunity to better understand the origins and earlier forms of our own behavior and to examine the emergence of our human intellect and spirituality. Most of all, we have an opportunity to behave better.

From this knowledge we must learn to accept the idea that *we can never wholly escape from our animal nature.* The medieval hermit in a dank and lonely hut by the Western Sea and the holy man with his rags and begging bowl in the dust and crowds of India are examples of humans trying to purge animal elements from their nature in order to reach spiritual purity. But the most extreme asceticism cannot overcome the chemical reality of our being and, try as he may, the holy man cannot wholly escape his animal biology nor change an atom of his DNA. Extreme asceticism ignores the valuable accomplishments which arose from and nourish the animal side of our nature. Do we really want to discard our sophisticated methods for procuring food, our marvelous buildings, our tool making skills, our medicine, our law, our games, and our sociability? We can never do that.

The message of this book is really very simple. Our human line separated from the same common ancestral line of the great apes approximately 5,000,000 years ago. For approximately 4,995,000 of those years, our behavior, like that of the other animals, was governed by biological need and emotion. Approximately 5000 years ago, after 99.9% of our existence up to the present time, a momentous event occurred in our intellectual development. We acquired a standard of behavior – Ethic! We also developed the ability to understand causation, leading to science. Only we have the intellectual capacity for this advanced way of thinking. *Human* behavior is now controlled by biological need, emotion, Ethic, and an understanding of causation expressed through experimental science. Those of us whose behavior is still controlled only by biological need and emotion remain pure animals. Because biological need and emotion are "hardwired" to behavior, it gives them stronger control over our behavior than the intellectual principle of Ethic. Being aware of this may help strengthen our intellect and provide the commitment required to more regularly behave like human beings.

In the end, we have no choice but to recognize and embrace the animal side of our nature *and direct it towards worthy goals through the genius of our uniquely human intellect and spirit.* The understanding of our recent and defining emergence as ethical beings requires the power of our intellect. But the commitment to ethical practice in each of our own individual lives requires the full commitment of our emotional spirit. Our true identity as humans is not the mythical purity of our vanity, but the living creation of our biological, intellectual, and spiritual development which we face everyday in the reflection of our personal lives. Thus we are, and thus we shall remain until the end of our time, and may Ethic guide us.

Epilogue and Dialogue

Don't tell me I am an animal

Epilogue and Dialogue

While in manuscript, this book was read by various people including one particular friend. She conscientiously read it over a period of several weeks, making valuable comments on various aspects of the work. When finished, she described her experience as being like "climbing Mt. Vesuvius." She explained that what she meant was that reading the manuscript required hard work, that as she progressed she frequently slipped backwards in her understanding of the ideas, and that on finally completing the task – reaching the top – the meaning became understandable. She never said why she specifically chose Vesuvius, but her subsequent comments about the message of the book have indicated that she sensed its explosive nature.

My friend's sensibilities to personal feelings and social interaction have always been acute and fine tuned, and her responses to the book were a valuable source of enlightenment to me on my success or lack of success with the ideas I am trying to convey. With her permission, I have recorded samples of a dialogue we had about a major message of the book.

The dialogue began after she had read the following passage I had just written. This passage was the result of a continuing evolution of my ideas on the emotional defense which is directed against the recognition of our continuing animal nature and of ways to constructively dismantle this defense. My friend's reaction and comments were so illuminating that I suddenly became aware of how badly I had failed to appreciate the intractability of the problem.

She read – "We are not pure humans. We never have been and never will be. We are still animals who have only just acquired an expanded intellectual capacity which – when we use it – makes us different. With our intellectual capacity, we are more than naked apes, we are unique among all life on earth. But despite the power of our intellect, our *shame at our continuing animal side* makes us blind. We are unable to see ourselves as being animals – at least in large part.

This is unfortunate because the continuing animal part of our being causes us much grief and suffering, while at the same time our blinding shame keeps us from understanding that this is the cause of our destructive behavior so that we can deal with it more effectively.

"Can we ever overcome this shame of being animal and begin to recognize what a remarkable event it was for us – alone of all life forms on earth – to have developed the intellectual capacity for expanded self-awareness, self-judgement, and ethical self-control? We take this event for granted as part of our blindness, our belief that we have always been pure humans with a conscience – a very dangerous assumption. Of what do we have to be ashamed? Can we not appreciate that we have experienced the most remarkable evolutionary event conceivable – we alone of the millions and millions of species that have existed on earth? But we do not. Our unshakable belief in the myth of human purity does not allow us to experience the wonder and awe that this extraordinary biological event deserves. Should we be ashamed that we alone show this spark of human understanding in a world of animal darkness? Can we not be pleased to be so fortunate? Can our ego and our vanity not be satisfied with this 'miraculous' appearance of intellectual capacity? Are we as a species really so egotistical and vain that we will accept nothing but purity? The supreme irony is that belief in human purity is an animal way of thinking. It disregards human understanding of causation on which is based our knowledge of the biological history of our species which clearly shows our continuing animal being.

"Also should we fear that accepting our dual nature – animal and human – prevents us from having religious faith or belief in a Supreme Power? Our intellectual development which makes us so special among all life on earth is so extraordinary that if anything, it would seem to encourage spiritual belief."

Friend - I have never thought like that.
I - What?
Friend - I have never felt any shame. I know we came from

I -   animals.
I -   I'm not talking about coming from animals, I am saying that you are an animal.
Friend - No! Damn it all, don't tell me that I am an animal! (My friend rarely uses profanity). We have gotten higher and higher. I'm insulted! You don't know what you are talking about. I'm superior! I'm better! I will not be lowered to an animal (beginning to cry).
I -   Why are you so angry? What is it about this that makes you upset?
Friend - I'm furious! You are hitting me in the gut! I have a conscience. Retaliation! (She later made some uncomplimentary remarks about me.)
I -   Do you think any part of you could be animal?
Friend - No! Maybe 1%. (We both laugh.)
I -   Is that the most?
Friend - Maybe 10%, but 90% is human!

    The next day, with her permission I read the section to her again as well as her comments of the previous day.

Friend - I don't have any shame. We have shown remarkable progress. We've climbed higher and higher. We have rockets. We have put a man on the moon. Our brains are so good. The things we've done – so overwhelming, mind boggling. Even landscaping a garden. Do you see a monkey putting a rock here and a plant there? (We laugh.) Don't tell me we haven't come far.
I -   Yes, but what I am saying is that the shame is unconscious. We are not aware of it.
Friend - I think you think we're stupid! I know how far we've come. How many thousands and thousands of years we've come. (Beginning to cry). Why do you keep talking about shame?
I -   I'm trying to understand what upsets you so about this.
Friend - I'm frustrated. I don't get it. I don't have any

shame. I'm not ashamed. Why am I ashamed? I look better than a fuzzy ape! (We both laugh and the conversation ends).

So there it was. I felt ashamed. I had put my friend through an unpleasant experience, and I had been blind to the real truth. But now I knew. I could see – but more importantly, *feel* – that, like my friend, my own emotion had permitted the idea of my animal origin – a less threatening belief. But, like her – and despite having written the book – I was still repelled by this horrible bombshell of an idea, this gagging, indigestible thought – *I am an animal.* Our conversation had exposed this very dangerous idea – "I am an animal." Not "I came from an animal." "I am an animal." That does it. That sets off the alarm. That is the message that cannot be received. The overwhelming threat of that message instantly overwhelms the intellect. Right now! All of the fine intellectual arguments, the logical niceties of the book are immediately vaporized – "Don't tell me I am an animal!" Forget it! I didn't hear! The end!

The overwhelming power of fear and shame. Shame, our invisible protector and our invisible enemy. Hardwired, all powerful shame. Ever on guard. What can human intellect do? The most powerful intellect which has evolved on earth. Only time will answer that question. Time to see if the knowledge we now have about ourselves can strengthen our intellect sufficiently to prevail in its currently unequal contest – the contest over recognizing the truth about ourselves. Or will we revert to a pure animal state as we often appear to be doing? Will this period of extraordinary self-awareness turn out to be only a splendid millisecond of cognizance, an aberrant spark of light in the long dark passage of evolution? The myth of human purity does not lend itself to this speculation but the reality of our evolutionary development does.

Sources of Information

To follow the truth wherever it may lead

Thomas Jefferson, 300 years ago
(4,999,700 HO)

Sources of Information

Some important sources of information for the ideas discussed in this book are described below.

Charles Darwin, *The Origin of Species*, Penguin Group, New York, 1958

The Origin of Species, which was published in 1859, describes Charles Darwin's theory of evolution. The acceptance of this theory is one of the turning points in human knowledge. Darwin has been characterized as ranking with the "great heroes of human *intellectual* progress."

In the introduction, Darwin characterized the book as "this Abstract," implying that he would address the subject in more detail at a later date. As it is, a modern paperback edition runs to 495 pages, and is densely packed with "facts" resulting from Darwin's, and others' observations on natural science. These facts are woven into the finely reasoned argument which Darwin used to convince the world of the correctness of his theory. As such, the book is tedious for the general reader to read from cover-to-cover. Darwin's introduction, which tells the story of how he made his momentous discovery, can be read with enjoyment by anyone interested in the history of human intellectual development.

The importance of Darwin's work to the current discussion is that it established the interrelation of all life on earth.

Jorge Yunis and Om Prakash. "The Origin of Man: A Chromosomal Pictorial Legacy" *Science* 1982; 215:1525-1530

This was the first study to use high-resolution technology to compare chromosomes from humans and the great apes. The close genetic relatedness of these species had originally been demonstrated by J. de Grouchy and associates using banded metaphase chromosomes. Yunis and Prakash found that humans and chimpanzees had 13 chromosome pairs which appeared to be identical while the remaining pairs were only slightly different. Their detailed comparative analysis of high-resolution chromosomes supported the idea of a common ancestor with a lineage from which gorillas separated first, followed by a divergence of chimpanzees and humans. The remarkable new knowledge of the extremely close genetic relatedness of humans and higher primates will forever shape the character of our self-awareness as a species.

Jane Goodall, *The Chimpanzees of Gombe. Patterns of Behavior*, The Belknap Press of Harvard University Press, Cambridge, MA, 1986.

Jane Goodall began her study of chimpanzee behavior in 1960. It was, she says, the fulfillment of a childhood dream of "studying animals in Africa." For over 30 years, she and her associates carefully observed and meticulously recorded the patterns of behavior of a band of chimpanzees living beside Lake Tanganyika. The book is 673 pages long and contains a large number of tables, figures, and pictures. Despite its length and scientific detail, it is interesting and understandable for the general reader. In addition to the scientific content, it tells the personal stories of the chimpanzees and their strivings to survive in their natural environment. One learns of their accomplishments, their failures, their physical and emotional illnesses, and their tragedies. One cannot help but come to know each member of the band by name and appreciate their good and bad qualities as individuals.

As a scientific work, *The Chimpanzees of Gombe* is of the first order. Its importance in this discussion lies not in what it teaches us about the chimpanzees, which is definitive, but in what we learn from it about ourselves. The descriptions of the never ending struggles for dominance within the group and of the violent assaults on chimpanzees from adjoining groups brings us two very clear messages. One message is the understanding we gain of the origin of our own continuing behavior. The other message – which is easier for us to accept through its description in another species – is what that behavior is.

NATURE (Producer, Fred Kaufman), *Monkey in the Mirror*, Thirteen/WNET, New York, 1995

The ingenious mirror technique for detecting self-awareness was first reported by Gordon Gallup in 1973 in a paper at the 9th International Congress of Anthropological and Ethological Sciences in Chicago. *Monkey in the Mirror* is a videotape that allows you to actually watch the process of self-recognition taking place as a chimpanzee views its image in a mirror. The amusing segment which shows the chimpanzee examining its teeth and eye and later trying to remove paint which has been applied to its forehead, leaves no doubt that the chimpanzee has developed self-recognition. The tape also shows a monkey playing a computer game with obvious concentration and, with what we are told, is good skill.

The intellectual capacity for self-recognition in a mirror separates humans and the higher primates from other animals. This ability is not present at birth and requires two years of intellectual development to appear. However, visual self-recognition by a naive adult is apparently not automatic without experience. Joseph Nagle, a sailor who went on a voyage to Australia in 1788, observed a native put his hand in back of a mirror to feel the person he saw in the reflection; in a way that he said was "equal to a monkey."

Michael Lewis, *Shame: The Exposed Self*, Free Press, New Brunswick, NJ, 1992.

This book describes pioneering studies of the development of self-recognition and self-conscious emotions in children. Observations of infant facial expressions and behavior indicate that children less than a year old can experience "primary emotions" such as sadness, fear, and anger. Intellectual development then leads to self-consciousness, as evidenced by self-recognition in a mirror, which begins around one-and-a-half years of age. During the second half of the second year of age, human self-awareness matures and gives rise to the "self-conscious emotions." These emotions are believed to arise only when the intellect has developed sufficiently to incorporate the concepts of *standards, rules,* and *goals*. This allows the individual to begin the process of self-evaluation. At this stage of development, children become able to show empathy, embarrassment, and envy. This is then followed by acquisition of pride, shame, and guilt at about three years of age. Lewis' findings are of very great importance in our understanding of the development of self-awareness and its effect on the human intellect. This book is 275 pages. It contains numerous examples from case histories, and is written in an easily understandable style.

Eliot Hearst. "Psychology and Nothing." *American Scientist* 79:432-443, 1991

As a source of interest to scholars and scientists, the subject of absence, deletion, and non-occurrence goes back to early cosmologists who puzzled over the emptiness of space. The animal experiments described in this short review provide a key source of information for understanding an important difference between animal and human thought. The inability of animals to recognize the concept of "nothing" means that *their thinking can only focus on the presence of something*. This limits their ability to make comparisons which depend on understanding the concepts of "more" and "less." We have called this the lack of an intellectual capacity to understand "reference." Understanding the concept of "nothing" along with having the knowledge of self-mortality are two features of human intellect which are not present in the thinking of animals. In the case of existence, it is obviously first necessary to know that you do exist before it is possible to know that you will not exist. It is interesting to speculate that these concepts are related, since understanding *absence* of one's own self is necessary for the recognition of self-mortality. Lower animals are neither aware of their own existence or of their impending non-existence. The higher primates have some degree of self-awareness but appear to show no evidence of an understanding of their own mortality.

Louis A Penner, et al. "The Lost Dollar: Situational and Personality Determinants of a Pro- and Antisocial Behavior." *Journal of Personality* 1976; 44:274-293

This is an example of an experiment designed to measure a form of honesty based on the criterion of returning a "lost" wallet containing money. In this experiment, involving psychology students, 45% of subjects returned the wallet, 37% ignored it, and 19% kept it. In other similar experiments, the percentage of "honest" and "dishonest" persons has varied according to circumstances, but the important finding is that a significant proportion of persons always fall into either the "honest" or "dishonest" groups. Various demographic, attitudinal, and personality variables have been examined to explain the difference in behavior, but the basic mechanisms controlling it are not understood. The lack of uniformity in behavior would not be expected if human behavior was rigidly controlled by the chemical reactions programmed by our DNA.

Hannah Arendt, "The Origin of Totalitarianism." Harcourt Brace & Co., New York, 1976.

This work of Hannah Arendt goes to the heart of understanding, destructive "human" behavior on a grand scale. The original manuscript of *The Origin of Totalitarianism* was completed in 1949. Nazi Germany and Hitler's concentration camps had been destroyed only four years earlier and the Russian Communist Empire and Stalin's gulags were still a terrifying reality. A third world war appeared to be an imminent possibility. Arendt characterized the period as being "like the calm that settles after all hopes have died." She wrote the book "out of the conviction that it should be possible to discover the hidden mechanics by which all traditional elements of our political and spiritual world were dissolved into a conglomeration where everything seems to have lost specific value, and has become unrecognizable for *human* comprehension, unusable for *human* purpose" (emphasis added).

The entire 527 pages of the book is worth reading for its historical perspective on totalitarianism, but what is most pertinent to the current discussion is Chapter 12, "Totalitarianism in Power." Arendt concludes that "the society of the dying established in the camps is the only form of society in which it is possible to *dominate* (emphasis added) man entirely." Again and again she returns to the subject of dominance and to her conclusion that this was the real purpose of the camps.

Another major theme of her book is the *unbelievability* of the horrors of the concentration camps and gulags, the inability of the normal human intellect to absorb the enormity of what was happening. The major theme of the current book is the value bestowed on our species from achieving *self-awareness*. As exquisitely painful as it is for us, becoming aware of the foulness and almost limitless destructive power of the continuing animal side of our nature is a new form of self-awareness that we must acquire and never lose. Reading Arendt's book helps develop this awareness.

Alfonso E. Pérez Sánchez and Julián Gállego. *Goya. The Complete Etchings and Lithographs*, Prestel, New York, 1995, pp 1-263

There are many books on Francisco Goya and his work. This one contains excellent reproductions of his "Black" paintings and of Los caprichos (The Caprices) and the Los desastres de la guerra (The Disasters of War). Francisco Goya was a remarkable man in several ways. His artistic skill as a painter places him among the first rank. Also, the acuteness of his political sense allowed him to survive the ominous dangers of the Spanish Inquisition, by which he was surrounded. But the full measure of his genius is found in the power of his intellect and its capacity for unwavering self-analysis of his species, an intellect which was strong enough to overcome the vanity, shame, and denial which mask the truth about ourselves. Added to this was Goya's courage to pursue this truth at a time when the dangers of public criticism and intellectual independence were very great.

The Disasters of War show shocking scenes of people

killing, mutilating, raping, and torturing each other; horrible in their graphic detail, full of animalistic fervor. They bring to mind the words we have invented to mask our destructive animal behavior, polite words for the ingenious ways we have invented to brutalize. Sophisticated "human" sounding words like "atrocity" and "violence" and "callousness." Goya did not use them in his captions which accompany the work. He was too honest. He just showed what happened – dismembered, naked bodies impaled on tree limbs – and paid little compliments – "A heroic feat! With dead men!" Goya's genius was such that his sardonic comments even made some of it funny! And it really is a joke, our history of egregious bestial behavior in the face of our unshakable belief in our human purity.

Los Caprichos looks at peaceful civilian life and addresses superstition, ignorance, vanity, deception, callousness, hypocrisy, greed, pedantry, corruption, and injustice. Like The Disasters of War, the underlying message is "human" inhumanity to "humans." We see the strong preying on the weak, witchcraft in action, institutional corruption, idle ignorance, and its all in good fun. And why not? Once we see the irony of our human condition as Goya did, it is hilarious. When Goya's work starts making you laugh, you are beginning to get the picture.

Robert Famighetti, Editor. *The World Almanac and Book of Facts 1997*, World Almanac Books, Mahwah, NJ, 1996

This reference is included because it contains an authoritative summary of dates of important events which have occurred since human emergence as a species. Having exact dates of events described in this book is not necessary – or even possible – for an understanding of chronology as it relates to the development of human intellect. What is important is that it be understood that important events in the development of our species have occurred during periods which were separated by orders of magnitude of time. Thus, the period of evolutionary separation of the human line, 5 million years ago, is quite different in time from the period 50,000 years ago which contains evidence for beginning ritual human burials and from 5000 years ago when Ethic is first recognized in human thinking. A clear understanding of the magnitude of these chronological differences is necessary for developing an accurate appreciation of the timing and pace of human intellectual development. Viewed on this extended scale, it becomes obvious that self-defining human intellectual development has just occurred. This is emphasized by the mathematical calculation presented earlier in the book which showed that 99.9% of our existence had no qualitative features which separated us from other animal species. Without this perspective, it is not possible to develop an accurate appreciation of our current emotional and intellectual strengths and weaknesses and of why we behave as we do.

Robert Fletcher, Suzanne Fletcher, and Edward Wagner. *Clinical Epidemiology. The Essentials*, 3rd ed., Williams & Wilkins, Baltimore, 1996.

Persons interested in understanding the principles on which science is based and ways of controlling chance and bias will find this a useful reference. This 246-page book was written as a text for students, but concepts are clearly explained and mathematical calculations are kept to a minimum. For the general reader interested in how experimental science works, the important thing to get from the book is to understand the *principles* of "statistical power," "control groups," "randomization," and "blinding." This can be learned from the book without having a mathematical background. However, for the general reader, the book does require careful reading and work. Also, obtaining help from someone with knowledge in this area would be useful in understanding the book. It is worth the effort because chance and bias not only affect scientific experiments but all of life in general.

Kenneth Rothman. *Causal Inference.* Epidemiology Resources Inc., Chestnut Hill, MA, 1988.

At the present time, very few people are exposed in school – at any level – to the subject of causality. This is in large part because most teachers also don't know about or understand the subject. This is not surprising since this understanding has appeared only very recently in human intellectual history. This 207-page book is a collection of 15 presentations which were made at a conference on Causal Inference. It is not surprising that the participants at the conference also did not totally agree among themselves on what were the essential elements of empiric "truth." "Truth" itself is a philosophical, not a scientific concept. What constitutes "truth" is based on belief, not scientific experimentation. There is no way to conduct an experiment which will establish what "truth" is in an abstract sense.

As discussed in the book, the late Sir Karl Popper proposed that the understanding of scientific truth was based on two elements, *predictability* and *testability*. In this process, prediction – an hypothesis – was made and then an experiment was conducted to test the idea to see if it were true. A good example of this is betting on a horse race. You decide which horse you believe to be the fastest. This is your hypothesis. You place your bet on it, and then the race is run. The race is the experiment. If your hypothesis is correct, you collect your winnings. It is argued in *Casual Inference* that a prior prediction is not an essential part of discovering the truth. After all, whether you pick a horse or not will have no effect on which horse wins the race. This is correct, but there remains an important practical issue.

For an experiment to be useful, you would like to have evidence that the results were correct and that you could apply them to future, natural events. That it has *external validity*. We have discussed earlier that chance and bias can cause an experiment to yield inaccurate results; therefore, the results of any experiment are always suspect. It is, therefore, desirable to confirm experimental results by further testing or by application of the findings to natural situations. In the example of the horse race, if your horse wins, by continuing to bet on it in future races, you might expect to win additional money, provided it faced similar competition. In the case of an experiment in physics, you would like to know that its findings allowed you to predict the cause of natural events which had not been previously explained. Therefore, successful prediction and confirmation, while not essential to the correctness of the original experimental result, do add another dimension to the confidence with which the new information can be accepted as knowledge. The more predictions which prove to be true, based on the new information, the greater the chance that causation has been accurately determined.

Index

Abbott, Robert, 42
abortion, 26
acquisitiveness, 9,10
activity
  complex, 11
  simple, 11
Adam and Eve, 22,116
adjective, 4,5
adventure, 89
adverb, 4,5
adversity, 71
alcohol, 83
altruism, 24
Analects, 24
anger, 12,13,15,16
animal
  activities, 9,10
  attitudes, 9,10
  behavior, 9,16,21,26,69
  characteristic, 8,9,10
  craftiness, 78
  goals, 15
  nature, 8,9,10,12,23,40, 121
  needs, 8
apology, 9,10
Arendt, Hannah, 88,131
arts, 89
asceticism, 121
aspiration, 6
assault, 9,11,30
  entertainment, 90
astronomy, 44,72
awe, 72

baby, 23
balance
  misleads intellect, 97,98
Barnum, P.T., 95
behavior, 62
  animal, 54,69
  destructive, 15,16,66,81, 124
  evaluation, 69
  experience, 50
  human, 54,57,58,59,61, 64,69
  options, 60
  pathologic, 80
bias, 35,37,39
biological
  basis, 12
  connection, 12
  need, 8,12,22,64,121
birth, 23
Blixen, Karen, 14
books, 103
brain, 1,112
Budd, William, 35
Buddha, 25,111
building, 8,9,10,54
bureaucracy, 41
  dangers of, 86,87,88
  dominance, 85
  nature, 85,86
  responsibility, 87
  vanity, 86
burial, 21,43,111

Index

camp, concentration, 87,88
cannibalism, 22
capacity, 9
caring, 25,64
causal inference, 49
  limits of, 58,112
causality, 9,11,21,49,78
  bias, 35,39
  chance, 35,39
  importance, 38,39
  logic, 35,36
  mathematics, 36
  prediction, 37
  romanticism, 100
  science, 35,36,49
  sensory perception, 34
  supernatural force, 34
  superstition, 35
causation, 3,20,116,121
celebration, 12
chance, 35,37,38,39
charisma, 76,101
charm, 70
children, 12,23,25,27,64,72
  Ethic, 31,32
  self-consciousness, 42
chimpanzee, 1,41,42,44, 71,72
  behavior, 118,119
  reference, 46
  technology, 55
chromosome, 1
Chung-shu, Tung, 66,71
civilization
  Ethic, 56
Cleisthenes, 75

close-mindedness, 9,10
cocaine, 83
common sense, 34
communication, 8,9,10
  artificial, 101
concern, 9,10
conditions, material, 16
Confucius, 25,67
conscience, 15,16,23,27, 51,70,116,118,124
  absence, 67,69
  awakening, 71,72,79
  bureaucracy, 87
  strengthening, 73
  working, 80
consciousness, 3,8,9
contemplation, 64
control, ethical 15
control group, 6,15
courage, 9,10,70
cow, 45
creation myth, 22
crime, 67
criticism, 108
Cro-Magnon, 112
Cromwell, Oliver, 108
cruelty, 69
culture
  Ethic, 56

da Vinci, Leonardo, 38
danger, 64
Darwin, Charles, 127
death, 21,31
  spirituality, 110
deceitfulness, 9,10
democracy, 75

Index

denial, 68
depression, 80
destroying, 9,11
Dhammapada, 25
difference, 6
Dinesen, Isak, 14
displaying, 9,56
DNA, 1,50
  behavior, 51
  function, 41
dominance, 10,14,41,64, 74,119
  pathological, 88
drinking, 8,56
drug
  abuse, 83
  addiction, 84
  mind-altering, 83

eating, 8,9,10,56
education
  graduate, 78
  human, 77
Einstein, Albert, 37
electronic mail, 103
embarrassment, 12
emotion, 8,9,10,12,16,22, 62,64
  animal, 13
  complex, 13
  complicated, 12
  control of, 15,70
  drug addiction, 84
  Ethic, 32
  faith, 113
  intensity, 98
  primary, 12

  romanticism, 100
  self-evaluation, 108
empathy, 12
entertainment, 89
  abuses, 90,91
  commercials, 90
  emotion, 89,91
  enlightenment, 91
  Ethic, 92,93
  intellectual content, 89
  power over intellect, 90
  self-awareness, 91
error, 9,10,108
Ethic, 7,9,11,26,28,49,63, 78,120,121
  animal behavior, 52
  appearance, 21,22
  children, 31,32
  civilization, 56
  components, 32
  culture, 56
  definition, 25
  education, 78
  emotion, 32
  fairness, 33
  faith, 113,114,115
  government, 76,82
  intelligence, 105
  nature, 29
  origin, 24,116
  practice, 30,31,33,66,70, 115,122
  romanticism, 100
  sophistication, 56
  wisdom, 105
  workings, 29

Index

ethical, 26
ethics, 24,26,27
eugenics, 16
euthanasia, 26
events, external, 64
evolution, 22,63,124
experience
  behavior, 50
experiment
  lost valuable, 51,64

fairness, 26
  Ethic, 33
faith, 39
  definition of, 112
  emotion, 113
  Ethic, 113,114,115
  judgement of, 115
  origin, 113
  religious, 124
Famighetti, Robert, 133
fashion
  Ethic, 94
  intellect, 94
fax, 103
fear, 8,12,126
feelings, 8,12,26
Fermet, Pierre, 38
fighting, 8,12,89
Fletcher, Robert, 134
Fletcher, Suzanne, 134
flight, 12
food, 8,119
force, 7
  external, 50
Frederick II, 25
Frederick the Great, 35

free will, 16
frustration, 16

Gállego, Julián, 132
games, 89
genes, 41
Genesis, 116
genetic engineering, 16
goals, life, 60
God, 25,62,113,116
Goodall, Jane, 128
gossiping, 56
government
  animal, 74,75
  Ethic, 82
  human, 74,75
Goya, Francisco, 91
  self-awareness, 92
grave goods, 21
grooming, 9
guilt, 10,13,14
  pathologic thought, 80

happiness, 8
hardwired, 12,15
hate, 8
Hearst, Eliot, 130
heredity, 66
higher primate, 1,21
history, 62
holocaust, 88
homo sapiens, 116
honesty, 9,10,25,64,69,72
  with self, 61
human
  activities, 9,10
  aspiration, 63

Index

attitudes, 9,10
behavior, 9,23,54,57,58, 59,61,64,69,121
characteristic, 8,9
dignity, 78
intellect, 8
nature, 9,20,118
purity, 62,80,100,118, 123,124
qualities, 8,21,71
humility, 10,72
hunger, 64
hypocrisy, 68

idea
  complex, 9,10
  simple, 9,10
  weight, 98,99
ideal, 6,24,48,106
  reference, 45
illness, mental 80
infant, 23,25
information, 37
  feature-negative, 46
  sources, 127
Inquisition, 114,115
intellect, 38,120
  emotion, 12,18
  faith, 113
  mind-altering drugs, 83
  pathologic, 81
  utopian paralysis, 106
  ways misled, 95
intellectual
  activity, 12
  capacity, 3,5,6,8,20,21, 24,25,45,118,123,124

content, 98
development, 27
force, 78
interaction, 102,103
maturation, 23
power, 6,120,122
intelligence, 105
internet, 103
intolerance, 9,10
introspection
  spirituality, 111
invention, 55,58

Jefferson, Thomas, 75, 81,97
Jesus Christ, 22,25,113
joy, 12
judgement, 6,9,11,20
  reference, 45
Judeo-Christian, 22,62,116

Kaufman, Fred, 129
Kierkegaard, Søren
killing, 11
Kipling, Rudyard, 95
knowledge, 37
Koffka, Kurt, 46

law, 7,67,78
leaders
  animal qualities, 76
  human qualities, 76
learning, 77
letters, 103
Leviticus, 25
Lewis, Michael, 3,13,129
liberality, 9,10

Index

lifestyle, 54
logic, 35
love, 8,25
Luke, 24
lying, 31,69
  entertainment, 90
  misleads intellect, 95
  television, 101
  to oneself, 96
  violation of Ethic, 30

machines, 54
magazines, 103
man-slaughter, 67
Markham, Beryl, 110
marriage, 119
mathematics, 36
media, 101
  intellectual interaction, 103
mirror, 3
Moses, 25
motorcycle, 55
murder, 30,67
myth, creation, 62,100,116

newspapers, 103
noun, 4,5
nucleic acid, 120
nurturing, 8,25

ontogeny, 22
open-mindedness, 9,10
opinion, 38
opportunity, 64
origin
  national, 64

tribal, 62

Paleolithic, 21
paralysis, utopian, 106
parenting, 8,9,10
Pascal, Blaise, 38
pathways
  chemical, 12
  nerve, 12
Patton, George, 106
peer pressure, 64,70
Penner, Louis, 131
Pérez Sáchez, Alfonso, 132
perfectionism, 106
philosophy
  definition, 39,112
  not testable, 58
  self-awareness, 44
phylogeny, 22
Plato, 66
playing, 8,9,10
post-modern age, 27
Prakash, Om, 127
prayer, 64
preposition, 5
pride, 10
Prince of Han, 67
probability, 38,42
psyche, 66
psychology, 38
punishment, 7,15,16,78
purity, human, 62,80,100, 118,123,124
purity code, 6

quality, 7,107

Index

race, 64
radio, 89,103
rage, 13,67
reaction, chemical, 50
reality
  pathologic thought, 80
reciprocity, 32
reference, 4,5,6,10,45
  absence, 46,47
  dogs, 47,48
religion, 21,34,43
  definition, 39,112
  not testable, 58
  self-awareness, 44
  standard of Ethic, 114
religious belief, 6,22
reinforcement
  negative, 16,17,78
  positive, 78
reproducing, 9,10
restraint, 15,16
reward, 78
rite, 6
risk, 107
robbery, 30
role model, 79
romanticism, 100
Rothman, Kenneth, 134

sacrifice, 22
sadness, 12
schizophrenia, 80,81
science, 3,6,9,11,20,21,35, 63,120,121
  definition, 36,39
  quality control, 37

self
  analysis, 20
  awareness, 3,4,8,10,11, 12,13,22,23,43,82,124, 126
  consciousness, 3,8,9,10, 12,42
  control, 16,124
  delusion, 26
  evaluation, 108
  judgement, 22,24,27,32, 48,66,81,116,118,120, 124
  mortality, 43,44,
  recognition, 3,43,71
sensory preception, 34,35
sex, 64,89
sexual reproduction, 8
shame, 10,12,13,14,15, 116,124,126
  pathologic thought, 80
shelter, 8
socializing, 8,9,10
Socrates, 38
solitude, 64
sophistication
  Ethic, 56
spiritual development, 120
spirituality
  definition, 112
  introspection, 111
  lack in animals, 111
  self-awareness, 110
  self-mortality, 110
St. Patrick, 72
standard, 6,7,9,11,14,22, 27,48,120

Index

behavioral, 26,121
personal, 14,24,31
reference, 45
stealing, 69
entertainment, 90
Stengel, Casey, 60
style
  Ethic, 56
suffering, 64
superstition, 34,35
system
  legal, 78
  political, 74

teaching, 9,10,77
  Ethic, 79
technology
  behavior, 54,55
  Ethic, 55
telephone, 103
television, 89,103
territory, 119
thinking, 38
  pathologic, 80
Thoreau, Henry David, 22
Thurber, James, 101
tolerance 9,10,58,106
tool making, 9,10,20,21
tools, 54,58
totalitarianism, 87
training, 9,26,27,77
  animal, 78
tranquility, 64
tribal origin, 22
truth, scientific, 26
truthfulness, 9,10,25,51,64, 72

tyrant, 81
Tzu, Chuang, 3
Tzu, Lao, 4

universe, 72

vanity, 14,62,122
verb, 5
violence, 16,74,89,119
voting, 75,76

Wagner, Edward, 134
war, 119
Washington, George, 108
water, 8
weapons, 54
wisdom, 105
wonder, 72
writing, 103
written record, 21,24

yang, 66
yin, 66
Yunis, Jorge, 127

zero, 47